INTRODUCING
PEOPLE
OF THE
BIBLE
VOLUME ONE

Also by John Phillips

Exploring Genesis
Exploring the Psalms
Exploring the Song of Solomon
Exploring the Book of Daniel
(by John Phillips and Jerry Vines)
Exploring the Gospels: John
Exploring Acts
Exploring Romans
Exploring Hebrews
Exploring Revelation

Exploring the Future
Exploring the Scriptures
Exploring the World of the Jew

Bible Explorer's Guide

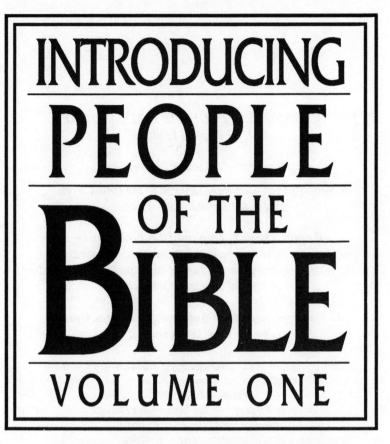

INTRODUCING
PEOPLE
OF THE
BIBLE
VOLUME ONE

JOHN PHILLIPS

LOIZEAUX BROTHERS
Neptune, New Jersey

INTRODUCING PEOPLE OF THE BIBLE, VOLUME 1
© 1991 by John Phillips

A Publication of Loizeaux Brothers, Inc.,

A Nonprofit Organization Devoted to the Lord's Work
and to the Spread of His Truth.

All Scripture quotations, unless otherwise noted, are
from the King James version.

Library of Congress Cataloging-in-Publication Data

Phillips, John, 1927–
Introducing people of the Bible / John Phillips.
ISBN 0-87213-627-2 (v. 1 : pbk.)
1. Bible—Biography.   I. Title.
BS571.P52   1991
220.9'2—dc20
[B]   91–39819

Printed in the United States of America

10 9 8 7 6 5 4 3 2

Contents

1
Adam, the First Man

Genesis 1:26-31; 2:7-8,16-25; 3:6-24;
Romans 5:12-15

I. ADAM AND HIS WORLD
  A. How God Created Him
  B. How God Cautioned Him
II. ADAM AND HIS WIFE
III. ADAM AND HIS WOES
  A. One Man's Disobedience
  B. One Man's Descendants

Think of the most handsome man you have ever met—handsome as a son of the gods. Think of the manliest man—the man with the most splendid physique, an athletic kind of man, keen of eye, muscular, coordinated and skilled. Think of the most brilliant person of whom you have ever heard—a Shakespeare, an Einstein, a Beethoven. Think of the man with the most spellbinding charm, the man with the greatest personality and charisma. That was Adam. Adam was fresh from the hands of God. Adam, in his unfallen state, was the crown of God's creation—destined by God to be the father of the human race. Adam was inhabited by God; he was man as God intended man to be.

I. ADAM AND HIS WORLD

It was a world of bliss and beauty, a world of harmony and peace. It was a world of perfect balance, where all the forces of nature were matchlessly poised. It was a world of glens and gardens, of mountains and meadows, of rushing rivers and deep, mysterious woods. It was a world like ours, but with nothing gone wrong.

A. How God Created Him

The Bible makes no apology for introducing God into the nature of things. The theory of evolution, which leaves God out of everything, is not so much a science as a propaganda offensive—a convenient tool in the hands of the atheist, the communist, and the humanist for postulating a universe without God. That is why the theory of evolution is so popular. It gives the unbeliever a working hypothesis for atheism. He can (at least to his own satisfaction) explain the universe without including God. Either the humanistic scientist is right or the Holy Spirit is right. The believer would rather trust the Holy Spirit than men's ever-changing opinions.

The Bible teaches that God made each creature that inhabits this planet as a separate order, species, or "kind." Each kind was separate from every other kind. Divine fiat created them. God simply spoke them into existence. When it came to the creation of man, however, God acted in a personal and distinctive way, making him by divine formation. God stooped down and fashioned Adam's clay. A great gulf exists between man and the animal creation.

God utilized the same general principle and pattern of creation, so far as man's body was concerned, that He had used for the animals. But God made modifications for Adam who was to be in His image and crowned as creation's lord.

The complexity of a functioning human body is a compelling argument against the theory of evolution. Suppose we were to try to make a human body. We would go to the store and bring home the raw materials: fifty-eight pounds of oxygen, two ounces of salt, three pounds of calcium, twenty-four pounds of carbon, some chlorine, phosphorous, iron, sulfur, and glycerin. We would now have our "do-it-yourself" kit; all we would need to do is put it together.

We would begin with something relatively simple—skin. In most places it would have to be paper thin and made to be stretched evenly over some eighteen square feet of the body. We would have to build into the skin some two million sweat glands to make sure that the temperature of the finished body would be kept within a degree or two of its normal 98.6 degree mark. Each sweat gland would have to be a tightly-coiled little tube buried in the skin's inner layer, with a one-fifth-inch-long duct rising to the surface. A piece of skin the size of a postage stamp would serve as a sample of the whole; it would require three million cells, a yard of blood vessels, four yards of nerves, one hundred sweat glands, fifteen oil glands and twenty-five nerve ends.

Something as relatively simple as skin is not simple at all. So how would we manufacture and assemble the ears, eyes, hands, and feet? And what about the blood, veins, arteries, kidneys, liver, heart, and stomach? What about an immune system? The complex disease of AIDS illustrates what happens when a person does not have one. This disease has baffled our best medical scientists for years.

Before we could begin making any of these organs, however, we would have to make some cells—a mere quadrillion of them (10^{15}). But to make just one cell would be an exercise of mind-boggling complexity. We would have to be

9

able to work on a very small scale, for the nucleus of each cell would need to be less than .0004 inch in diameter. The components of the cell would have to be enclosed in a membrane only .0000005 inch thick. The core would have to contain the genes and chromosomes, and we would need to imprint these with the "master plan"—the blueprint or "code of life" containing all the information necessary to determine whether the cell would be that of a cockroach, a camel, a horse, or a human being. This would involve arranging some twenty amino acids in an almost endless order to make the awesomely complicated assortment of proteins needed to build the body.

Another thing we would have to keep in mind: every minute some three billion of these cells would die, so we would have to arrange for them to be replaced at that rate.

And so the calculations go on. To believe that all this astounding complexity evolved by chance is to believe the impossible. Evolution is the atheist's inadequate "explanation" for the universe. It explains nothing. For example, add up all the component parts in a body. Remember that each one has to be in its right place at the right time, flawlessly performing the function for which it was designed. The odds against all this happening as a result of the blind working of the forces of chance are about the same odds against *Webster's Unabridged Dictionary* resulting from an explosion in a printing plant.

So we return to the Biblical account of creation. God created Adam. God set him apart from the rest of creation and gave him a *spirit*—something He had not given to bird or beast, fish or fowl. God made it possible for man to be inhabited by Himself; man in his nature, person, and personality could live, move, and have his being in fellowship with God.

An animal does what it does because it is what it is. It acts and behaves the way it does because of what we call *instinct*. Nobody has to teach a salmon to seek out the river of its origin in order to spawn and die there. The salmon does what it does because it is what it is—a salmon. Nobody has to teach a spider to weave a web. The spider weaves a web the way its mother wove a web—by instinct. Nobody has to teach a bee to build a hive with hexagonal chambers tilted at the correct angle to the sun to keep the hive at a constant temperature. Nobody has to teach a bee to maintain a colony with exactly the right relationships between the queen, drones, and workers. Nobody has to teach a bee how to locate nectar or how to pass the word to the colony. All this work is done by instinct. A bee does what it does because it is what it is.

In other words, the governing principle in a creature—whether it be an insect, a four-footed mammal, a fish, or a bird—is instinct. The creature is locked into a special pattern of behavior by the wisdom and power of the Creator. Some of the higher creatures show signs of personality and manifest an ability, within limits, to learn. They exhibit such emotions as joy and sorrow. In other words, they may have what we call a *soul*. Even so, instinct controls their behavior.

God could have created man the same way. We could have been created to do what is right by instinct, but then God would have only had another breed of animal—a superior breed, but still an animal. Instead, God built into man a different governing principle. He gave man a *body* to make him world-conscious, a *soul* to make him self-conscious, and a *spirit* to make him God-conscious. In man, the body was to be governed by the soul—by the intellect, emotions, and will. The soul, in turn, was to be governed by the spirit, the new ruling principle that sets man apart from the beasts. The human spirit was to be indwelt by the Holy Spirit, so that man—in fellowship with God, indwelt by God—would do, say, and think in harmony with God.

B. How God Cautioned Him

In order for man to be a self-governing, rational, morally accountable, volitional being—a *person*, not a *puppet*—he must have the power of choice. He must also be placed in an environment in which that power of choice can be exercised.

So when God planted the garden of Eden, He placed within it the tree of the knowledge of good and evil.

In effect He said, "Do you see that tree, Adam? That one is Mine. You can go where you like in the garden. All things are yours to enjoy richly, except for that one restriction. That tree is Mine, and you are not to eat of it. If you do, you will die. Now, then, enjoy your world."

II. ADAM AND HIS WIFE

The Holy Spirit intends the story of Adam's love, courtship, and marriage to be the divine prototype of all love, courtship, and marriage. The boundless freedoms, the experimentation, and the trial-and-error system of our modern world find little or no approval in the Bible. When Jesus spoke the last word on the question of divorce, He added this significant statement: "All men cannot receive this" (Matthew 19:11). The same is doubtlessly true concerning the divine pattern of love, courtship, and marriage found in Genesis 2. There we see illustrated the divine ideal, although not everyone has the grace to be governed by it.

In the beginning, Adam was celibate and was happy and content to be single. He went about his work in Eden, enjoyed daily fellowship with God, and lived a full-orbed life as a single person. He was engrossed in the hundred and one things that made up his daily life. He had evening times of communion with God and went to bed conscious of a need for nothing. Then God awakened in him a sense of lack.

God brought the animals to Adam to receive names. The purpose behind this stimulating, highly complex, mental exercise was to make Adam fully conscious of something: every animal had its mate. He alone, of all God's creatures, had no one his equal with whom to share life's joys. So Adam became acutely aware of a missing dimension in his life. For the first time, he was lonely.

Then God put Adam to sleep, and he went to sleep in the will of God. Doubtless Adam had committed this whole area of his life—his missing love life—to God. He did not run frantically all over Eden, beating the bushes to find someone to fill this newly discovered longing. He went to sleep in that "good, and acceptable, and perfect" will of God. Such reliance on God is wholly foreign to most people in our western world. Our ideas of love, courtship, and marriage are molded more by movies and fiction than by any thought that God might have a better way. This is largely true even when the single person is a believer and anxious to marry a believer. Dating is our pattern; dependence on God is the Biblical pattern.

When Adam awoke from his trustful rest, it was to look into the face of the woman God had created especially for him. If Eden had been a paradise before, it was ten thousand times a paradise now.

Then Adam spoke his vows: "This is now bone of my bones, and flesh of my flesh" (Genesis 2:23). During the days that followed, the couple lived in the wonder of an Edenic honeymoon. Every day they discovered something astonishing. Every day Adam took joy in introducing Eve to a new marvel in that pristine paradise. In the cool of the day, hand in hand, they sought their daily quiet time with God.

So Adam was now happily married in the will of God. He was married to Eve whom God had designed to bring love and companionship, life and color, into his already glorious life. Such is God's ideal marriage. The Lord Jesus referred to this idyllic scene when He made His authoritative pronouncement on divorce. He endorsed the ideal.

III. ADAM AND HIS WOES

The idyllic conditions of Eden that could have lasted forever suddenly ended.

A. One Man's Disobedience

The Bible clearly speaks of Adam's sin. Actually, Adam was not the first to sin; Eve was the first. But God held him accountable. God always holds the man accountable for what happens to his wife. Adam, the ordained head of his home, was responsible before God for his wife's spiritual welfare. This principle still holds true today.

As Scripture records, the serpent entered Eden. It was not the serpent Adam had known from the day of his creation. It was not a beautiful, graceful creature named and known by Adam for its cleverness. It was "that old serpent" (Revelation 12:9; 20:2), an invader who came in the guise of a serpent with the express purpose of infecting the human race with the virus of sin. He found Eve alone, deceived her, and left her in nakedness and shame. Already shadows were gathering in the garden of Eden.

Adam found her, lost and alone, standing before the tree of the knowledge of good and evil, holding the forbidden fruit. She did not have to tell him what she had done; he knew. She was disturbingly different. Her beauty had a different, sensual quality. When she held out the fruit to him, there was allurement in the act—a mixture of provocation and pathos that struck a false but tantalizing chord.

We can picture Adam's consternation. He loved her, and now she was lost. Nobody had to tell him that. He knew it intuitively from the indwelling Holy Spirit. He knew the word of God: "The day that thou eatest thereof thou shalt surely die" (Genesis 2:17). He was about to lose this woman whom he loved—lose her forever. He loved her more now that he was about to lose her than he had ever loved her before in her sweet innocence. He was not deceived. The Bible clearly states that Eve *was* deceived and that Adam was *not* deceived. His keen intellect took in the situation at a glance, weighed all the factors in the equation, and arrived at the correct answer. His wife now knew good and evil. Moreover, in learning about evil she had become evil. Between Eve and Adam a gulf now existed as deep and as wide as that which separated the rich man from Lazarus in our Lord's teaching (Luke 16:19-31).

A door had slammed irrevocably on the past. Adam and

Eve could not go back to the idyllic Eden they had known. Eve was no longer innocent; she was guilty. She was no longer pure in mind, heart, and will. She was tainted and depraved. At once she had become both a sinner and a seducer. She was tempting Adam at that moment. She knew it; he knew it.

We do not know how long Adam debated the issues within himself, weighing all the factors in his brilliant mind. We only know the decision that he reached. His great love for Eve led him into sin. His heart went out to the woman he loved. His *logic* said, "No! No! A thousand times no!" His *love* said, "Yes! Yes! Ten thousand times yes!"[1]

As Eve had followed her *head* into sin, so Adam followed his *heart* into sin. He looked again at Eve—at his beloved wife, at the companion of so many blessed, blissful days. She was lonely and afraid. He could see the haunted look in her eyes. She was now under God's curse. Soon He would be abroad in the garden. Then would come His sentence—death!

Well, Adam decided to share her sin and sorrow. With one almost magnificent gesture, eyes wide open to the consequences, he took the proffered fruit from her hand, deliberately bit into it, tasted its bittersweet flavor, and became a *sinner*. He deliberately stepped down to where she was.

Thus, as Paul put it, "By one man sin entered into the world, and death by sin" (Romans 5:12). One man's disobedience ruined the human race.

B. One Man's Descendants

When Adam fell, all creation fell. We were all "in Adam" when he fell. He dragged the entire, unborn, human race with him into sin.

No sooner had Adam sinned than the light went out in his soul. His next act was one of folly. He made an ineffective,

---

[1]Adam was not deceived; he was disobedient. He knew what he was doing and his love for Eve was the only possible motive. His love for her, which should have been subordinated to his love for and trust in God, had become idolatrous. From a purely human view it seemed noble.

foolish effort to cover the nakedness of which he had just become aware. He sewed fig leaves together to cover his shame and the shame of Eve.

Thus false religion was born, for such an act is the essence of all false religion—man's attempt, by his own effort, to cover the guilt and shame of his sin in order to appear acceptable to God.

Adam's fig leaves served well enough for him and Eve, but the leaves were woefully inadequate in the presence of God. Adam and Eve had to learn that "without shedding of blood is no remission" (Hebrews 9:22).

Soon God's judgment fell; the gates of the garden clanged ominously behind the fallen pair. Now they faced a future in which no thought, word, deed, incident, accident, motion, or motive could be divorced from the terrible fact of sin. Nor could they forget that the only road back to God was by way of the shed blood of Calvary's Lamb.

Adam was not long in discovering what kind of seed the serpent had sown into the world by his fall. Adam himself was no longer inhabited by God; he was inhabited by sin; the controlling principle of the indwelling Holy Spirit was gone. And Adam's sons were born in sin and "shapen in iniquity" (Psalm 51:5). Sin leaped full grown on this stage of time.

Adam's first son, Cain, grew up to be a murderer. Cain, Scripture reveals, was very religious, but his religion was too refined to slay a lamb. However, his religion was not too refined to slay his brother Abel, of whom he was jealous. Abel disagreed with Cain's religious creed, but his simple trust in God and acceptance of God's way of salvation won Abel God's approval. Infuriated, Cain murdered Abel. Then, far from being repentant before God, he was insolent.

Adam lived for 930 years (Genesis 5:5). We do not know how many of those years he lived in Eden. Perhaps he lived there for thirty years, since Jesus (the Second Man) was thirty years old when He met the same old serpent with far different results.

In any case, Adam lived on and on in that world before the great flood. He saw evil men and seducers wax worse and worse. He saw harvest after harvest of wickedness reaped on the earth. He saw his oldest son establish an utterly godless civilization. He saw the knowledge of God linger for a generation or two in Cain's family and then die out altogether.

Adam also saw his sons' astonishing inventiveness. He saw them found great cities and discover the art of smelting. He saw them bring the world through an industrial revolution that changed the course of history. He saw man's cleverness with cattle. He saw arts and entertainment come into being, flourish, and reach full fruition on the earth. What din and noise it all was after the peace and quietness of Eden.

But side by side with all this splendor and achievement was unparalleled wickedness. "Every imagination of the thoughts of [man's] heart was only evil continually" (Genesis 6:5). Adam saw the rise of a pornographic society in which lust, lewdness, and license reigned supreme. It must have broken his heart. Indeed, by the time Adam was several hundred years old, he must have been the unhappiest man who has ever lived.

One redeeming factor remained—the godly remnant of Seth and his sons. Adam did not live to see the full fruit of their goodness, but when he was 622 Enoch was born. Sixty-five years later, when Adam was 687 Enoch began to walk with God. That must have tremendously encouraged Adam. Just 57 years after Adam died, Enoch was translated to Heaven. There he and Adam have been walking with God ever since. There Adam, Abel, and Seth wait for the coming of you, me, and the last of Seth's godly line.

2
Eve,
Mother of Us All

Genesis 2:18–3:24; 4:1-8; 5:1-3

She was as fair as the morning, bright as the day, warm as the sunshine, and as sweet as honey in the comb. She was the essence of womanhood. She was brimful of life. Her husband lost his heart to her the moment that he saw her. Her name was Eve.

If we each think of the most beautiful woman we have ever met—a woman with grace and charm, wit and personality, charisma and appeal—Eve personified that woman.

I. EVE'S FUTURE

Normally when we meet someone attractive, we like to know something of his or her past. Eve had no past; all she had was a future.

A. Her Maker

God was her Maker. On this point even the so-called theistic evolutionist faces an insurmountable controversy with the Bible. The theistic evolutionist tries to accommodate the evolutionist by conceding that Adam could have evolved under God's directing hand. But what about Eve? There is no way she could have evolved. The Bible says that God created Eve from Adam's side as a special, final act in the creative process. This is either true or false. If the Bible is true, then evolution is false. If evolution is true, then the Bible begins with a gross, inexcusable mistake. Both views cannot be true. Here in Genesis 2 we have fact or fable—one or the other.

Moses hinted that Eve was almost an afterthought with God. Again and again in Genesis 1, the creation chapter, we read, "And God saw that it was *good"* (italics added). At the end of the chapter we read, "And God saw . . . it was *very good"* (italics added). Then, after placing Adam in the garden, God said: "It is *not good"* (Genesis 2:18, italics added). "It is not good that the man should be alone; I will make him an help meet for him." God went on to produce His masterpiece. He created a woman whom Adam called Eve.

Matthew Henry said of Eve that God took her from Adam's side—not from his head to rule over him, and not from his feet to be trampled on. God took her from Adam's side to be his equal, to be protected under his arm, and loved close to his heart.

One moment there was no woman. The next moment she stood before him: fresh from the hand of her Maker, with no past, with only a future.

B. Her Marriage

The first thing that happened to Eve after her creation was her wedding. There was a lightning-swift courtship when God introduced Adam to her. They met. They married. Just like that. And instantly Adam's paradise became a double paradise.

Jesus goes back to this Edenic scene when He states His sublime views about marriage (Matthew 19:1-8). Let us note that. Jesus believed in a literal Adam and Eve. If the evolutionist is right, then Jesus was wrong. It's unthinkable for anyone to claim to be a Christian and accept the view that Jesus, the incarnate Son of the living God, could be wrong about anything. During His earthly stay, Jesus was never wrong about anything. He is the eternal, uncreated, self-existing, second person of the godhead. He stepped out of eternity into time to be born as a man among men. While always never more than man, at the same time Jesus was never anything less than God. He was God manifested in flesh. As such, He was omniscient in His wisdom. He made no mistakes. Anyone who says that He did is a deceiver and an antichrist.

When the disciples asked the Lord to expound His views on divorce, He took them back to the beginning of creation. He went back beyond the prophets, beyond Sinai, right back to the garden of Eden, back to this first wedding. He, Himself, had officiated at this wedding as the father of the bride and friend of the bridegroom. Divorce, Jesus taught, had its roots in human hardness; marriage had its roots in divine love. "What therefore God hath joined together," Jesus stated, "let not man put asunder" (Mark 10:9). That was His verdict.

So Eve was created and Eve was married. Before her

stretched an eternity of bliss in an earthly paradise. She and Adam lived in ideal surroundings. They had the delightful task of tending and keeping that Edenic garden. It was filled to overflowing with exotic fruits and flowers; it was graced by all kinds of birds and beasts, each one perfectly tame and wholly submissive to their will. There were wide rivers to explore, forests to roam, and surprises and delights at every twist and turn. Their days were full of wonder; their nights were filled with starry skies. The cool of each day became a special time when God came down to the garden to walk with them, to talk with them, and to open up before them new and marvelous mysteries of His handiwork in Heaven and on earth.

Then one day the serpent came.

II. EVE'S FALL

The serpent was none other than fallen Lucifer, who was using the graceful serpent's form. Evidently he waited until Eve was alone.

The Bible tells us much about this old serpent. Three chapters in from the beginning of the Bible, we meet him for the first time. Three chapters in from the end of the Bible, we meet him for the last time. In between we discern his evil trail. Before his fall Lucifer was "the anointed cherub"—the greatest, most glorious, most gifted, and most gorgeous of all the creatures God had made. Lucifer was the choirmaster of Heaven, brilliant in appearance, and the highest of all created intelligences.

After his fall, he retained great gifts of genius, only now they were bent, twisted, and warped. His soul was soured by sin. He was driven by an implacable hatred of God and by an all-consuming envy of the human race. He came into the garden of Eden to spoil. His one great passion was revenge. He wanted to bend, twist, and ruin the human race because man had been made in the image and likeness of God. That image Lucifer desired above all else to deface.

On the surface of things, Eve was no match for this evil one. The Holy Spirit tells us that he was full of subtlety. Eve, in contrast, knew nothing of sin. She had never been tempted. All she had was the armor of innocence and the Word of God. But in herself she would be no match for the fallen Lucifer. If it came to discussion and debate, he could beguile her in no time.

Besides, God had intended her to be the heart of things, not the head of things. He had created, ordained, and commissioned Adam to be the head, not Eve. Her first mistake was in not calling for Adam, her federal and spiritual head, as soon as temptation began.

Even so, there was no reason why Eve should have fallen so easily into Satan's crafty snare. She had one weapon he feared—the Word of God. Of course her Bible was quite small indeed, consisting of just two verses (Genesis 2:16-17). But that would have been enough. One word from God, believed and obeyed, is a mighty sword.

To all the serpent's wiles, Eve simply would have had to say, "Thus saith the Lord." All she would have needed to do was fall back on God's inspired, inerrant, invincible Word and she would have been safe. It was all the protection she would have needed. Had she drawn and used that Sword, fallen Lucifer—stabbed and pierced through and through, his soul screaming with the cut and thrust of that Sword, his wounds burning and flaming from its fires—would have fled in mortal terror from the garden, from the planet, from the solar system, and from the galaxy. He would have put a million light years between himself and that Sword.

But look at what happened. In the first place, Eve was clumsy in her use of the Sword of the Spirit. She used it, it is true, but she misused it. She constantly misquoted it, she subtracted from it twice, and she added to it once. She thought that she could paraphrase it and improve it. She thought that as long as she had the general drift of God's thoughts in mind, the actual words did not matter. She set up her puny mind as

23

the ultimate authority as to what God had said and what God had meant. Therefore she was putty in the devil's hands. Likewise, there is no hope today for the man or woman who thinks that the Bible can be handled like that. They are the devil's dupes from the beginning.

We are not going to labor here over the cut and thrust of that battle—for a battle it was, with the stakes being the rule of the world and the ruin of the human race. We will simply note that Satan challenged the Word of God along three lines.

A. The Challenge

He first challenged:

1. The Authorship of the Word

"Yea, hath God said . . . ?" (Genesis 3:1) Lucifer was, in effect, asking, "How do you know that God said it? Maybe Adam said it. What proof do you have that it is *God's* Word?" Of course, if there is doubt as to the authorship of the Bible, there is a question as to its authority. "Yea, hath God said . . . ?" Nobody has answered that Satanic challenge better than Dryden the poet. With his open Bible before him, he wrote:

> Whence but from heaven
> Could men, unskilled in arts,
> In different ages born,
> From different parts
> Weave such agreeing truths?
> Or how, or why
> Should all conspire to cheat us with a lie?
> When—starving their gains
> Unwanted their advice,
> Unasked their pains
> And martyrdom their price?

Next Lucifer challenged:

2. The Accuracy of the Word

"Yea, hath God said, Ye shall not eat of every tree of the garden?" The evil one was asking, "How do you know that the words you quote are exactly what God said? How do you know that there is no error in the transmission of this 'word' of God? After all, you weren't there when it was given. All you have is what has been handed down to you. It may not be inerrant after all."

Then Lucifer challenged:

3. The Acceptability of the Word

After listening to Lucifer, Eve saw that the forbidden tree "was good for food, and that it was pleasant to the eyes, and a tree to be desired to make one wise" (Genesis 3:6). "Why should anyone," he was suggesting, "place such a restriction on you? After all, you are a mature adult. You should do your own thing. As an intelligent, thinking, independent person, you should simply not accept such a narrow restriction being placed on your behavior."

Because Eve did not have a firm grip on the authoritative, inerrant, divinely inspired, Holy-Spirit-preserved and God-revealed word of Scripture, she was an easy prey for the tempter.

One moment she was free, magnificent, God-obeying, Bible-believing, and Spirit-exalting. The next moment she was a temptress and a seducer, determined to drag her nearest and dearest down to her level.

The sun still shone brightly in the sky. The flowers still shed their perfume. The four rivers still flowed out of Eden. But there was a difference. The alluring serpent had vanished, and the light of the Holy Spirit had gone out of Eve's soul. The Holy Spirit no longer indwelt her spirit. She was suddenly much more aware of her body and very much alive to all kinds of wickedness. Her imagination was quickened to things suggestive and seductive, and her soul was tinged by the first shadow of coming night. Instead of delighting her, thoughts of God disquieted her.

Eve had not anticipated that the knowledge of good and evil would be like this. It was both frightening and fascinating. Moreover, she had suddenly become a schemer. Deep within her, the light that had previously illumined her soul and bathed her body in a rainbow robe had gone out. She was naked. She knew that she had become evil. She did not like it and wanted to do something about it, but she did not know what to do. Her sense of exposure filled her with a desire to run away and hide. She experienced shame. A terrifying thought haunted her: *What will I do when God comes?*

God had said, "In the day that thou eatest thereof thou shalt surely die" (Genesis 2:17). *What did that mean?* she wondered, her fears rising. Eve already knew that something had died within her and she did not like it at all. She was suddenly greatly afraid of God; she was a sinner, and would become the mother of a whole race of sinners.

Maybe Adam would help her. But how could she explain to Adam what had happened? How could she tell him how she now felt? How could she describe this tumult of emotions that now surged in her soul? The scheming part of Eve decided at once that Adam must become like her. Then he would know what she knew. Then he could bring his magnificent intellect to bear on the problem of nakedness, exposure, guilt, and fear.

B. The Change

Notice the four downward steps in her fall:

1. She Saw: The Look Became a Lust

There are certain things we cannot help but see, things on which we ought not to look. They are the very stuff of which temptation is made. The glance *starts* the fire; the gaze *stokes* the fire.

2. She Took: The Desire Became a Decision

She was now in the throes of temptation. She held the forbidden fruit. She was deliberately playing with temptation, toying with the forbidden fruit.

3. She Did Eat: The Choice Became a Chain

Satan can pander to our desires. He is the "super-pimp" of the universe. He can procure, propose, and pander, but he cannot push. But the moment Eve ate, she became a slave. She committed sin, and as Jesus said, "Whosoever committeth sin is the servant of sin" (John 8:34).

4. She Gave: The Sinner Became a Seducer

It is a proven fact that people who are entangled in the snare of an evil habit, an enslaving lust, or an unquenchable craving, will try to get others to join them in their sinful actions. Eve was no different. It did not take weeks, months, or years for all her sin to develop. Sin sprang full-grown into her soul. She was no sooner a sinner than she was a seducer.

Nobody has to learn how to be a sinner. Nobody has to be taught how to tell lies, how to be self-willed, how to throw a temper tantrum, or how to indulge the lusts of the flesh. We are all very good at sinning—quite naturally.

Eve woke up that morning in fellowship with the angels of God, at peace with the world, and a daughter of Heaven. She went to bed that night a sinner, very much alive to the knowledge of good and evil. She became a slave to sin and a stranger to goodness.

III. EVE'S FAMILY

For the rest of her days, Eve's life revolved around two focal points.

A. A Messiah

Her dreaded confrontation with the holy God was not long in coming. But lo! God, true to His character, tempered government with grace, law with love, ruin with redemption, and punishment with promise. For even as He pronounced sentence, He pronounced salvation. He promised that a Messiah would come from the seed of the woman, no less. There would be a serpent seed, but God would also provide a special seed. One day from the woman (not from the man) One would come who would trample the serpent, give His precious blood to cleanse mankind, provide His righteousness as a robe for their souls, and restore the lost splendors of Eden.

Eve believed that. In fact, when her first son was born, she cried out with joy, "I have gotten the Man, even Jehovah!" She was wrong in her conclusion but right in her conviction. She thought Cain was the promised Christ. He turned out, though, to be more like the seed of the serpent than the promised Savior seed.

Cain was a clever little boy, but he was also very contrary, and cruel. Eve had to cope with his temper tantrums, with his pride and self-will, with his lies, and with his downright disobedience. We wonder how she managed to cope with all that.

By the time her second son was born, Eve knew her mistake. She called him *Abel*, which means "vanity." One thing she was sure of: Cain was not the promised Savior seed. She reacted to this disillusionment by registering her disappointment, doubt, and discouragement in selecting the name *Abel*.

B. A Murderer

The two boys grew up. Abel was a genuine believer; Cain was merely religious. Then one day Abel disappeared.

"Cain, have you seen Abel?" we can imagine Eve asking.

"No, I don't know anything about him," he responded. "Why should I? Am I my brother's keeper?"

Shortly after that the terrible truth came out. Cain had murdered Abel. Cain had murdered him in a fit of rage and resentment over Abel's faith in God. Branded and accursed of God, Cain packed his bags and left home—defiant to the last— to become the world's first city-builder and to found a great but utterly godless civilization. The civilization was so godless that before it ended, its evil called down the flood tides of God's wrath on the earth.

Who but a mother can measure the heartache and sorrow that Eve carried with her to the grave as a result of that terrible tragedy? She had reaped a bumper crop of the harvest of her sin.

But what a woman she was, after all. We can picture her one day, not long after the tragedy, listening when Adam said, "Well, Mother Eve, I guess that's about it. Two sons—one a martyr, the other a murderer!"

But Eve answered, "No, that's not it at all. I'm going to have another son. I'll call him *Seth*, which means 'the appointed one.' You see, dear husband, I was not wrong about the *truth* of the coming seed; I was just wrong about the *time*. I still believe in God. I challenged His Word once, and Cain and Abel were the result. I shall never challenge His Word again."

So in due time Seth was born and became the founder of the royal line to the Messiah. After the passing of many centuries, One came of whom we read:

God, who at sundry times and in divers manners spake in time past unto the fathers by the prophets, Hath in these last days spoken unto us by his Son, whom he hath appointed heir of all things, by whom also he made the worlds; Who being the brightness of his glory, and the express image of his person, and upholding all things by the word of his power, when he had by himself purged our sins, sat down on the right hand of the Majesty on high (Hebrews 1:1-3).

3
Elimelech, the Backslider

Ruth 1:1-5

I. A FALLEN MAN
  A. A Confession
  B. A Connection
  C. A Coronation
II. A FALSE MOVE
III. A FORBIDDEN MARRIAGE
IV. A FAMILY MORGUE
V. A FINAL MISTAKE

The story of Elimelech is a Biblical classic on the high cost of backsliding. Despite all his professions of faith, Elimelech took the reins of his life into his own hands. He became a backslider in Moab and sowed the seeds of all the sadness and sorrow that followed in his life. Indeed, the first chapter of Ruth is dark with tragedy. Tears flow in rivers. All is chaos and darkness. And this all resulted because Elimelech was a backslider.

It has been well said that the first call from God to a person is this question: *Heaven or Hell?* One has to decide how he wants to spend eternity. He can spend it as a child of God and joint-heir with Jesus Christ in the mansions of glory; he can be saved by sovereign grace, washed in the soul-cleansing blood of the Lamb, and regenerated by the Holy Spirit; his name can be written in life's eternal book. Or he can spend eternity forever lost in the blackness of darkness, cut off from God and His grace in that terrible place where there is weeping, wailing, and gnashing of teeth. That is the first question: Heaven or Hell?

The second question is similar. Once a person decides that at all costs he wants to go to Heaven, a second question surfaces: Which world are you going to live for, Heaven or earth? This question arises in the story of Abraham and Lot in the Old Testament and in the sad case of Demas in the New Testament. It is tragically possible for a person to have a saved soul and a lost life, to see one's whole life as a Christian go up in smoke as wood, hay, and stubble at the judgment seat of Christ—to be saved "so as by fire" (1 Corinthians 3:15).

There seems to be little doubt that Elimelech was a genuine Old Testament believer. But he lived for the wrong world, and he paid a very high price for that in both his own life and his family's lives.

Five things come into focus when we think of Elimelech.

I. A FALLEN MAN

Our first consideration has to do with his remarkable name. Almost everyone familiar with the Bible knows that Biblical names, particularly Old Testament names, are of great significance. The name *Elimelech* was no exception. It means "My God is King," and it tells us three important things.

A. A Confession

Look at the center of that definition. What do you see? The words *God is*. Elimelech carried that truth around with him to his dying day.

It is significant that the Holy Spirit begins the Bible with the grand assumption that God is: "In the beginning God created the heaven and the earth." There is no attempt to prove that there is a God, just the bare assertion: "God created."

We, of course, might have wanted to suggest half a dozen lines of reasoning to prove that there is a God. We might have started an argument using the clear evidence of law and order in the universe (law and order that seem more intricate and marvelous the more we study various scientific disciplines). Then we might have concluded that the universe could not have formed by chance.

For instance, millions of complex factors make up one living, functioning, human body; the idea that it could be the end product of chance is ludicrous. We could put the parts of a watch in a washing machine and slosh them around for a hundred billion years and they would never assemble themselves into a watch.

But the Holy Spirit makes no attempt to demonstrate the fact that God is. Like the writers of the American Declaration of Independence, the Holy Spirit deems that certain truths are self-evident.

So we have Elimelech's confession: God is. Elimelech was not an atheist or agnostic. He adopted the key position later enunciated by the Holy Spirit: "For he that cometh to God must believe that he is, and that he is a rewarder of them that diligently seek him" (Hebrews 11:6).

Elimelech's name also shows:

B. A Connection

The name embodies a personal pronoun. It does not just mean "God is"; it means "*My* God is." Somewhere along the line, the living, self-existing God of the universe had become Elimelech's personal God. His testimony was simple: "The God who is, is my God." For Elimelech, God was not a remote, infinite, impersonal being, who having created the universe simply tossed it into space and left it to its own devices. He was a God who permitted, encouraged, and even sought a personal relationship with members of the human race.

This is another marvelous truth about God. He has revealed Himself. He wants us to know Him. Even more important, He wants to belong to us and He wants us to belong to Him. This is the clear teaching of the Bible. In the opening part of John's Gospel we read this remarkable statement: "As many as received him, to them gave he power to become the sons of God, even to them that believe on his name: Which were born, not of blood, nor of the will of the flesh, nor of the will of man, but of God" (John 1:12-13).

In other words, the God who is, can become my God. I can accept God into my life by inviting the Lord Jesus to come and, by His Holy Spirit, take up permanent residence in my innermost being. Many people will affirm that God is; not many can say that they have established this vital connection with God.

C. A Coronation

"My God is King." That is also part of the revelation of God in the name *Elimelech*. Indeed, how could God be anything less?

According to what Elimelech professed through his name, there had been a time when he had crowned the true and living God—the Creator of the universe, Elohim-Jehovah, the God of creation and the God of covenant—as *Adonai*, the God of control. He had handed the legislative, executive, and judicial roles in his life over to God.

God cannot accept anything less. In Luke 6:46 Jesus said, "Why call ye me, Lord, Lord, and do not the things which I say?" He also told the story of the foolish virgins (Matthew 25). They came and knocked on the door of the house after they missed the coming of the bridegroom. "Lord, Lord, open to us," they said. He replied, "I know you not."

It is possible for a person to profess faith in Christ and not, at once, recognize that he must hand over all aspects of his life to Jesus. The believer may not learn at once that the Lord Jesus has the right to reign and rule in his heart. But if the professing believer never learns that and never makes any attempt to give Christ His proper place, possibly that person does not know Christ at all.

There is a great deal of theological debate about the place of the lordship of Christ in conversion. It is possible for a person, like Elimelech, to give Christ His proper place once and then take back, into his own hands, the governing reins of his life. Some people, however, say that Jesus is their Lord and yet have missed salvation completely. There can be no greater tragedy than to discover at last that Heaven's door has been shut and to hear the Lord say that He never knew you. The best thing to do is to make sure of our salvation.

As we look at Elimelech, we see a man who by his very name claimed to have made a confession, a connection, and a coronation in his life. "My God is King!" he seemed to be saying.

But even as the story opens, we see that he was a fallen man. He was saying all the right things and doing all the wrong things. And that can only spell disaster for any man.

II. A FALSE MOVE

"A certain man of Bethlehem-judah went to sojourn in the country of Moab, he, and his wife and his two sons" (Ruth 1:1). Notice the Holy Spirit's use of the *polysyndeton*—the repetition of the word *and*. It indicates a deliberate, significant, step-by-step happening. The journey was also a false move.

The name *Bethlehem-judah* means "house of bread and praise." Symbolically, Bethlehem is the place where God meets the needs of a starving world. To Bethlehem, indeed, He sent the Bread of Life from Heaven. Bethlehem is the house of bread, the house of praise. In other words, Bethlehem is a type[1] of the local church, the New Testament "house of bread and praise." Here God's people gather to feed on the bread of Heaven and offer praise to God.

Now we can recognize Elimelech's false move. He left Bethlehem-judah. He left the place where God had put His name, the place where God met the needs of His own, the place where God's people offered praise to Him. If Elimelech were living today, we would say that he left the local church, the gathering place of God's people.

Elimelech, of course, had good reasons for leaving Bethlehem-judah—at least they seemed like good reasons to him. There was a famine in the land, and even God's people were suffering.

Elimelech's solution to the problem was typical. He left. Probably he did not make a fuss about it. Very likely he simply said, "There's not much here for me. My family isn't getting fed. I'm leaving." That was his big mistake.

He should have stayed and allowed God to do something for him there and, indeed, something through him there. He should have allowed God to be God in his life. He should have said, "There has to be a reason for this dryness and barrenness. I want to be part of the solution." Instead, he quit.

How often have we met people like Elimelech? They leave a local fellowship after finding fault with the preacher, the elders, or some of the others. Everyone who wanders away from the local church thinks he has a good reason. Instead of saying, "There is a problem here, there is a famine of the Word of God among His people here, but I'm going to let God work through me to turn things around," they leave. As often as not, they end up in Moab. They finish the course of their lives by going nowhere, by joining a church with flawed doctrine, or by completely immersing themselves in the world.

Moreover, backsliding never takes place in a vacuum.

---

[1]Webster defines *type* as "a person or thing (as in the Old Testament) believed to foreshadow another (as in the New Testament)."

Backsliding always involves other members of the family. Elimelech's wife was involved, as were his two sons. Of the four who went to Moab only one was ever spiritually recovered.

Elimelech should be renamed. Instead of being called "my God is King," he should be called "I am king." We now see a man completely out of touch with God, His Word, His people, and His Spirit. He made a false move.

III. A FORBIDDEN MARRIAGE

We do not know how old the sons were when the family moved to Moab. Probably they were teenagers, at least. Here is the Holy Spirit's comment through Scripture: "They came into the country of Moab, and continued there" (Ruth 1:2). Perhaps there were more job opportunities in Moab. Perhaps someone offered Elimelech better pay in Moab. Doubtless he only planned to stay there until the situation improved in Bethlehem.

The sad fact was, however, that Elimelech continued living there. Likewise, it is far easier for us to continue a course of backsliding than it is to return to the house of bread and praise. To return involves making the verbal or unspoken confession: I made a mistake.

So Elimelech's sons grew up in Moab. During their most impressionable years, when they were forming their most important friendships, they were thrown into contact with an exotic, sinful world. They grew to manhood outside that protective boundary where God draws His own circle around His own.

One day Mahlon brought a girlfriend home. Her name was Ruth. She was lovely, but she was a Moabite—a stranger to God and His Word. Their friendship developed into marriage. So now one of Elimelech's children was thoroughly married to the world.

Before long the other son, Chilion, did the same. Now both of Elimelech's sons were "unequally yoked together" with unbelievers and committed to a Moabite way of life.

The names of these two young men are significant. The name *Mahlon* means "sickly"; the name *Chilion* means "pining." The Holy Spirit intended for these names to indicate their spiritual condition. One son was weak; the other was wistful. And no wonder. Neither grew up in the kind of spiritual atmosphere that would have developed a robust faith. Elimelech could talk about God's truths as much as he wished (and no doubt he did), but the example he set undid everything that he said. Why shouldn't the sons settle in Moab? Their father had. If they found *marital* compromise with the world acceptable, it was because their father had found *monetary* compromise with the world acceptable. Likewise, we cannot bring up our children in a worldly atmosphere and then complain because they have worldly appetites.

Elimelech must have known that God's Word was crystal clear on this matter. "Neither shalt thou make marriages with them. . . . For they will turn away thy son from following me . . . so will the anger of the Lord be kindled against you, and destroy thee suddenly" (Deuteronomy 7:3-4). And it happened—even more dramatically because God's special curse rested on Moab. "An Ammonite or Moabite shall not enter into the congregation of the Lord; even to their tenth generation" (Deuteronomy 23:3)

These marriages, then, were forbidden by the law of God, but Elimelech seems to have written that legislation off as so much narrow-mindedness. In the East parents arranged marriages and were quite involved in drawing up the contracts. By now Elimelech was so far backslidden, had lost control over his sons to such a degree, and was so much the victim of his circumstances that he actively helped to arrange these marriages. That was the final nail driven into the coffin of Elimelech's backsliding. He lost his family in Moab. It was bad enough that he became a backslider, but look well at what he did to his sons.

IV. A FAMILY MORGUE

"And Elimelech Naomi's husband died. . . . And Mahlon and Chilion died also both of them" (Ruth 1:3,5). The family was in Moab for a scant ten years, but the tragedy of unbelief and backsliding had struck long before death came in. God's displeasure was quickly demonstrated.

First we have the death of Elimelech, whose name meant "My God is King," but whose every breath in Moab was a repudiation of the testimony of his name. The life of the backslider is a lie. When God is no longer a person's king, his life has little meaning. The whole purpose for which he was created in Adam and recreated in Christ is annulled.

God left Elimelech alone for a while to see if, like the prodigal son, he would come to his senses and return to Him. This Old Testament prodigal never did that. Perhaps he liked Moab; probably he became too involved in Moab. It is amazing that in our day believers who will not become involved in the church are willing enough to become involved in the world's clubs, associations, leagues, and societies. Thus these believers advertise to their children exactly where their true values lie—in the world.

So God waited, but Elimelech showed no sign of repentance and return; he just continued his daily routines and settled down in Moab. He became a willing exile, far from the place where God had put His name, far from the place that, despite its drought and difficulties, was the one place in all the world where God met with His people. There in Moab Elimelech died—out of fellowship, a backslider.

That first funeral in Moab was a direct word from God. It was a terrible, tragic, and unmistakable word. God intends that every funeral we attend should cause us to search our hearts and examine our ways. The dead person lying in his coffin preaches his last sermon, for better or for worse, to those who have been left behind.

How dark it was. No one in Moab read a comforting Scripture to the sorrowing family. No one came in and prayed with the bereaved. Their neighbors doubtlessly dropped in to pass on a few pagan platitudes, but that was all.

The death of their father, however, did not speak to either Mahlon or Chilion. Mahlon should have said to his younger brother, "You know, Chilion, we need to get back into fellowship with God's people. Dad always said that he was not going to die in Moab. He often told us about Jacob and Joseph and how they wanted to be buried in Canaan. Let's take our father's body and go back to Bethlehem—back to the house of bread and of praise." But no, only silence reigned. Or maybe, if Mahlon did speak like that, Chilion replied, "My wife would not come, and even if yours would, what kind of reception would she receive from God's people?"

Both Mahlon and Chilion died in Moab too. They died young, as they had lived, with no interest in spiritual things. The family morgue was busy those days, as the death angel came again and again. God spoke once, again, and yet again, and always in the same stern voice.

V. A FINAL MISTAKE

We read of Naomi: "And the woman was left" (Ruth 1:5). This statement is so brief that we tend to hurry past it in our Scripture reading. But it is the last despairing signpost on the highway of the backslidden man. *Left.* In Moab. Left in the company of the ungodly, far from God's people. Left to shift for herself with two sons in a place where God had never intended them to be. That is the last blot on Elimelech's life, and a very black blot it is.

So he died and was buried and angels carried him to

Abraham's bosom. But we can well believe that, unlike Lazarus, poor Elimelech would not be comforted. Like the rich man in Hell who could only think of his brothers, Elimelech could only think of his boys. We can imagine a conversation between Abraham and Elimelech in Heaven.

Abraham might say, "Can't you be still, Elimelech?"

"Oh, Father Abraham," Elimelech might reply, "I have two sons. Send Caleb; send Joshua."

"They have Moses and the prophets, so let your sons hear them," Abraham would respond.

"But oh, Father Abraham, I neglected to nurture them spiritually and failed to ground them properly in the truth of Moses and the law. I was too concerned that they receive a good education in Moab, that they attend the best schools, and that they make the right business contacts. Maybe if someone rose from the dead, they would believe."

"If they don't believe Moses and the prophets," Abraham would say, "neither will they believe if someone rose from the dead. They have their Bible. God has no other word than that."

So poor Elimelech tossed and turned. His sons lived like pagans in Moab, and they died like pagans in Moab. Now poor Elimelech has nothing to look forward to but the coming judgment day when God will call him to account for the way that he lived and the influence that he wielded.

Again, we can almost reconstruct the scene at the judgment day: "Well, Elimelech, so you are here. Where are those two boys I trusted you with in Bethlehem-judah, in that house of bread and praise?"

"Alas, Master, like Abraham I commanded my children and my household. He commanded his children in Your ways; I commanded mine in the ways of the world. I took them to Moab, Lord, and I left them there. I lost them there."

4
Naomi, a Backslider Restored

Ruth 1:8-22; 2:19-22; 3:1-5

Elimelech, the Old Testament's prodigal, died in Moab, far from the promised land. Unlike the New Testament prodigal, Elimelech was content to sit down and eat the husks that the swine ate.

Some backsliders are like that. They know the Lord. They are not dogs returned to their vomit or sows wallowing in the mire. They are sheep, but they are wandering sheep. We can be sure that Elimelech never did the evil things that the

Moabites did. He did not worship their terrible gods. But he made no attempt to get back to Bethlehem-judah, where God had put His name.

Naomi was different, and it is with her that we are concerned here. She received restoration with truly wonderful results.

I. HER PLIGHT

What a serious plight Naomi was in, to be a widow and a foreigner in Moab. Let's look at the inhabitants of that land to gain a clear picture of her environment.

The Moabites and the Ammonites were descendants of Lot. During two nights of drunkenness and incest mentioned in Genesis 19, Lot—the great backslider of his day—spawned two terrible foes of God's people, Ammon and Moab. The Ammonites were descended from Lot's younger daughter, the Moabites from Lot's older daughter.

The Ammonites represent in Scripture the sinful world's open and undisguised *hostility* to God's people. They were a wild, nomadic race, often in league with the enemies of God's people.

The Moabites, on the other hand, were more settled and civilized. They did not fight against Israel; they were more subtle. Moab hired a false prophet to curse God's people and sent women to seduce God's people. Balaam's advice was simple. In effect, he said, "You cannot *subdue* them, my lord king, so *seduce* them. Don't rely on the men of Moab; rely on the women of Moab." (See Revelation 2:14.)

In Scripture the Moabites represent the sinful world's *hospitality* to God's people. The world is always a dangerous place for believers, but never more so than when it offers us the right hand of friendship and fellowship. The world says, "Come and join us. Join our lodges, our clubs, and our fraternities. Come and enjoy our lifestyle. It is much more free and open than yours. Come and compromise with our gods. We do not demand that you worship them—just that you do not preach against them."

This was the Moab in which Naomi now lived, a lonely widow. It would be hard to imagine a more dangerous place to which a man could lead his wife and family or a more perilous place in which to leave them.

The chief god of the Moabites was Baal-peor, probably another name for Chemosh, who was worshiped on the summit of mount Peor. The god Chemosh was cruel, like Moloch, and people worshiped him with horrible rites. Little children, for example, were sacrificed in the fire to Chemosh. How a genuine believer could *not* preach against that kind of evil activity is hard to understand.

In the Mosaic law, God set up a special barrier against the Moabites. No Moabite, as we saw in Deuteronomy, was to be permitted to have a share in the worship of God until his tenth generation.

During the days of the judges, the Hebrews, because of their sin, were allowed a taste of Moabite rule. Eglon, the fat and repulsive king of Moab, oppressed them for eighteen long years. If nothing else, *that* should have warned Elimelech of Moab's true nature.

But Elimelech, as we have seen, was a backslider, and backsliders rarely pay much heed to the Word of God even when they know its facts and precepts by heart.

So we note *Naomi's plight.* She had been abandoned in Moab. Her plight was all the more difficult because her sons had cemented their backsliding by marrying into Moabite families.

Naomi's name means "pleasant," which suggests that she had an attractive disposition. She had been pleasant to know and be around, but backsliding changed all that. When she finally arrived back home in Bethlehem, people hardly recognized her. They said, "Is *this* Naomi?" (Ruth 1:19, italics added) Notice her reply: "Call me not Naomi, call me Mara: for the Almighty hath dealt very bitterly with me" (1:20).

Naomi used a rather interesting name for God—the name *Shaddai*, which means "the Almighty." *Shaddai* does not mean "the God of creation," or "the God of the covenant," but "the God of contentment." He is the God who will "supply all your needs according to his riches in glory by Christ Jesus" (Philippians 4:19). Elimelech had denied this aspect of God's character when he moved to Moab simply because there was a temporary famine among God's people. He thought that God had let him down and that the world would treat him better than God. And now Naomi blamed God for her sad state: "Shaddai, the God of contentment," she said in effect, "has let me down." It is extraordinary how people blame God for the troubles they bring on themselves. "Call me not Naomi, call me Mara." Backsliding had turned her into a bitter old woman.

II. HER PLAN

"She had heard in the country of Moab how that the Lord had visited his people in giving them bread" (Ruth 1:6).

This is an Old Testament way of saying that the people of Bethlehem-judah had experienced what today we would call a revival. God had made His presence felt, and Bethlehem-judah had again become "the house of bread and praise." God's people were feasting on both the living bread and actual, physical bread.

Yet Naomi was living in a far country, perishing with spiritual hunger. She was surrounded by starving millions who never so much as knew of a place like Bethlehem where God visited His people and gave them bread. All they had tasted was the bitter bread of Baal-peor.

A great longing sprang up in Naomi's heart, a deep desire to return to the house of bread and praise, to go back to the fellowship of God's people. She did not know how much longer she would live, but she did know that she did not want to die in Moab, out of touch with God and far from the place where He spread a table for His own. All Moab had ever given her was a place to bury her dead.

One day Naomi announced the news to her two daughters-in-law, her only real friends in Moab. "Orpah and Ruth," she said in effect, "I'm going to say goodbye. I'm going back home, back to Bethlehem-judah, back to the God of my youth." The two women decided to go with her.

III. HER PLEA

We observe that all three women took the first steps together: "Wherefore she went forth out of the place where she was, and her two daughters in law with her; and they went on the way to return unto the land of Judah" (Ruth 1:7). Often one person's decision to get right with God influences other people.

There was, however, a great deal of difference in the attitudes of these three women. Naomi was a backslider coming back to God. Ruth was a genuine convert who made a life-transforming decision. Orpah was an inquirer who started well but did not follow through; she came forward, so to speak, but that was all there was to it.

Orpah never did make it to the promised land. We are not going to develop that side of the story here, but we must note that she turned back and we must lay much of the blame for that tragedy on Naomi.

Picture these three women heading toward the Moabite frontier. We can see Naomi and Ruth in earnest conversation as Naomi told her about the God of Heaven, the God of the Hebrews; Naomi told the stories of Abraham, Isaac, Jacob, Moses, Joshua, and the conquest of Canaan; she told Ruth about the law, the offerings, and the feasts. Then suddenly they missed Orpah. They turned around and there she was, far behind, looking back toward her childhood home. She was thinking of all that she was giving up and leaving behind.

They went back to her and then Naomi, still in her backslidden condition, gave the two women terrible advice: "Maybe you'd better not come with me after all. You see, girls, you'll not have much chance of getting married again in my country. Indeed, I can't think of a single self-respecting Jew who would marry a woman from Moab. No Jew living within the boundaries that God has drawn around His people would marry you. You'd have a much better chance of getting remarried if you stayed down here in Moab."

Here two young women had shown initial interest in the truths of God and had taken the first steps toward life's most important decision. All Heaven and Hell swung in the balance for these Moabite women, and what did Naomi do? Did she try to engage Orpah's affections toward the living God? Did she urge Orpah not to look back but to go on? Did Naomi say, "Remember Lot's wife"? After all, the Moabites were descended from Lot.

No. She poured cold water on their incipient faith. She talked to them about getting married, as if that were the all-important goal in life. Indeed, she waxed eloquent on the subject. She said all the wrong things. Trust a backslider to do that.

Then Naomi's terrible eloquence bore fruit. The women hugged, shed tears, and the moment of decision came. We can picture Orpah straightening up and hear her saying, "You're right, Mom. I know some nice young men in Moab, and I do want to get married again. I can't stand the thought of remaining single all my life. I'm going back."

Back she went—back into spiritual darkness, back to the demon gods of her people, back to Moab. And we read of her no more. In later years Naomi may have awakened in the night and thought of Orpah down there in Moab. She may have touched her cheek and felt the place where Orpah had kissed her. She may have thought of Orpah going to a lost eternity— thanks to the advice she had given.

It is a terrible thing to have another's soul on one's

conscience. Yet how careless we are in a backslidden state. We say things, we do things, we influence other people, and we barely give a thought to the results. We help to push someone a little further down the broad road that leads to destruction and do not lose a moment's sleep.

Then, through God's grace, we may regain a right relationship with God. But there are still people whose feet are firmly fixed on the wrong road, who hurry on toward endless pain because of something that we have said or done. And what do we do? We yawn in the face of God and go on as though there were no great white throne for lost sinners and no judgment seat of Christ where He will review and judge the deeds that believers have done. What must God think of our adamant hearts and our cast-iron consciences?

The Holy Spirit does not record that Naomi was ever bothered about Orpah. We would like to think that she was. However, nothing is said. No prayer for Orpah is recorded. No wish is expressed that some traveler from Judah might make a bypass through Moab and look Orpah up. Nothing.

There are other examples. Think of Abraham and Lot. Through Abraham's backsliding in Egypt, Lot developed a taste for this world. Because the well-watered plains of Jordan looked "like the land of Egypt," Lot moved down there. Abraham never forgot that it was largely his fault that his weak nephew developed a taste for backsliding. Abraham rescued him once. And when Lot went back to Sodom a second time, Abraham pursued him with prayer. Indeed, the very night that Lot fled to the hills to escape the doom of Sodom and then fell into those terrible sins that produced an Ammon and a Moab, Abraham was praying for him, pleading with God for whatever righteous souls might be found in that city of sin.

IV. HER PLACE

The Holy Spirit does not tell us of all the adventures and discouragements that marked Naomi's journey home. But at last, after considerable time, she began to see the fields and farms of her native Bethlehem. She was a widow, she was poor, and she had been away for a number of years. But she had now come back home—back to the place where God always intended her to be. We note four things about Naomi, now living in the place of blessing instead of the place of backsliding.

A. Her Fellowship

"And it came to pass, when they were come to Bethlehem, that all the city was moved about them" (Ruth 1:19). The restoration of this backslider caused quite a stir among God's people. Everyone in Bethlehem was talking about it. "Naomi's back. Have you seen her? She's looking terrible. She's glad to be back, but she has paid a high price for backsliding." We can imagine how the tongues wagged. They always do. That is a part of the price of restoration to fellowship. There will always be those who are thoughtful, considerate, and Christlike, but there will always be others who gossip. The prodigal son, for instance, had his elder brother to face. Unfortunately the church has its share of such narrow-minded people. But the important thing was, Naomi had returned.

This story points out great differences between the Old Testament and the New Testament. In the Old Testament, all blessings were connected with a *place;* in the New Testament, they are connected with the *person* of Christ. In the Old Testament, one had to be in *Canaan;* in the New Testament, one has to be in *Christ.* In the Old Testament, everything had to do with being in the *land;* in the New Testament, everything has to do with being in the *Lord.* In the Old Testament, the Jew who moved out of the land was out of the place of blessing and fellowship—the place where God had put His name—because all God's blessings were "yea and amen" in Canaan. (See 2 Corinthians 1:20.)

Thus in Ruth 1, all is sadness. The family expected to

profit from going to Moab; instead it reaped nothing but sorrow. But now Naomi was back in fellowship with God's people, back to where the songs of Zion were sung, back to where the Word of God was known, back to where God's people were daily reminded of Calvary, back to where the table was spread, and back to where God took up His place in their midst. What did Moab have to compare with all that? "I went out full," Naomi sadly admitted, "and the Lord hath brought me home again empty" (Ruth 1:21).

B. Her Fruitfulness

Naomi did not have any sons to carry on the family name. What sons she once had, she had lost in Moab—a terrible place to lose them. When will we ever learn the high cost of backsliding?

But although Naomi had no sons, she did have a daughter. Naomi had become a soul-winner. She had brought a poor, lost pagan under the shadow of the wings of the Lord God of Israel (Ruth 2:12).

How quickly Ruth—this new convert—grew in the things of God. We can be sure that at first many Jews viewed Ruth with suspicion. The people of God do not always welcome new converts with open arms, especially when they come from a wholly pagan background. Christians should welcome them, but sometimes they don't. There are cliques in many churches. It can be quite difficult for a newcomer, especially if he is from a "suspicious" background, to gain acceptance. All too often our churches are refrigerators rather than incubators. But Ruth persevered.

It wasn't long before the people were saying to Naomi, "Thy daughter in law, which loveth thee . . . is better to thee than seven sons" (Ruth 4:15). That was quite a testimony.

And Boaz took note of her too. He said, "All the city of my people doth know that thou art a virtuous woman" (Ruth 3:11). What better fruit could one want than that?

C. Her Fragrance

We remember that when Naomi first came back into the fellowship, she was a bitter old woman. "Call me Mara," she said. But it wasn't long before the quiet influence of the place of fellowship wrought a change in her. As a result the people again called her *Naomi*—"pleasant."

That is what a right relationship with the Lord and His people will do for us. It will change us, make us more Christlike, and make us pleasant to be around. If that is not happening, something must be very wrong with our relationship with the Lord and His people.

One fruit of the Spirit is joy. The world offers many things, including pleasure and all kinds of amusement, but it cannot offer joy. Joy is much greater than happiness. Happiness depends on what happens; joy transcends circumstances. The Lord Jesus—that great Man of Sorrows—constantly spoke of His joy in the upper room, with Calvary's shadow already dark upon His soul. The Bible says that a person who is filled with the Spirit will express it "in psalms and hymns and spiritual songs, singing and making melody in [his] heart to the Lord" (Ephesians 5:19).

Only sin can spoil a believer's joy. After his sin with Bathsheba, for example, David did not lose his salvation, but he lost the joy of his salvation.

So, then, Naomi had her fragrance restored to her. Instead of shedding gloom everywhere she went, she shed gladness. People began to notice her joy. They discovered that she was a pleasant person to be around. They gave her back her old name—Naomi. We must notice that in the Spirit-filled temperament, love, joy, and peace are predominant characteristics. May the Lord lend us His fragrance so that we may advertise an attractive brand of Christianity in this gloomy, sinful world.

D. Her Future

What future did Naomi have in Moab? Judging by the experience of her husband and her sons, the only future she had was a grave. Time was getting on, she was getting older, and misery was her constant companion. But once she was restored to God's people, once she returned to the place of blessing, her future was restored.

That is how the story of Naomi ends. Ruth gave birth to a baby boy, and the women of the village put their heads together and named the little fellow *Obed*, which means "worshiper." The Holy Spirit, however, did not stop there. He went back to Pharez, the son of Judah, and counted eight generations to Obed. And the Holy Spirit did not stop there either. He counted two more generations to David—ten generations altogether.

The Holy Spirit thus linked together grace and glory. He went back to the time of Pharez because it was then that God exhibited *grace* to the house of Judah—undeserved grace, overruling the circumstances of Pharez' birth. He went on to the time of David because it was then that God exhibited *glory* to the house of Judah. In Obed, Naomi's future was secured. We can trace that future as it runs from Obed to Jesse and on to David. Later the Holy Spirit added other names until the names springing from little Obed culminated in the name that is above every name—Jesus!

So Naomi's future was restored. God gave her a future beyond her wildest dreams when backsliding in Moab. Through her grandson Obed, God gave Naomi a living link to Jesus. What more could a person want?

The Lord restored to Naomi "the years which the locust [had] eaten" (Joel 2:25).

When we walk with the Lord in the light of His Word,
What a glory He sheds on our way!

While we do His good will He abides with us still,
And with all who will trust and obey.

Trust and obey, for there's no other way
To be happy in Jesus, but to trust and obey.

(John H. Sammis)

5
Ruth,
a Pagan Seeker

Ruth 1:4-22; 2:1-23; 3:1-18; 4:10-17

I. RUTH AND THE SOVEREIGNTY
   OF GOD
   A. Drought - A Famine
   B. Discovery - A Family
   C. Death - A Funeral
   D. Dismay - A Fear
II. RUTH AND THE SALVATION
   OF GOD
   A. A Roused Soul
   B. A Redeemed Soul
   1. Ruth Meeting Boaz
   2. Ruth Marrying Boaz

Ruth was a Moabitess, a member of an accursed race. She was born and bred in paganism. The gods of her people were fearful, filthy, demon gods. We can well imagine that when Ruth was little, she would sometimes catch her parents whispering together in fear: their tones hushed, their eyes watchful, their faces grave. She would catch a word or two to add to the little store of information that children collect about the adult world. We all know how children do it; we have done it often enough ourselves. They add two and two together until they know more than their parents give them credit for. Soon Ruth knew that her parents' fears centered on the priests.

The priests of Moab were powerful and cruel, and they served an assortment of gods. But the most feared god of all was Chemosh, or Moloch. Chemosh had his terrible place among the gentler gods on a platform of movable stones under which great fires could be kindled. Chemosh's lap was so constructed that little children placed on its red-hot surface would roll down an inclined plane into his fiery belly while slaves kept fresh fagots heaped on the hungry fires.

When disaster threatened Moab—plague, famine, the possibility of war—the priests called for another burning. They would come around the homes to inspect the children for possible victims, looking especially for firstborn sons. With a red dye obtained from the seashore, they would stain the wrists of designated victims. There was no court of appeal from the priests' decision. Children with stained wrists were doomed to horrible deaths.

Perhaps when Ruth was a child, she would hear her parents whispering about this and her heart would be filled with dreadful dreams that would be transformed into nightmares.

When Ruth was old enough to play with other girls, she heard about another god—actually a fertility goddess who offered the Moabites regeneration through the gratification of lust with harlot priestesses in the temple. The fertility of fields and farms, people believed, depended on the sex orgies in her temple.

Just as the priests always kept their eyes open for firstborn sons that could be fed to Chemosh, they kept their lustful eyes open for promising girls who could be conscripted for the foul trade of the temple. Ruth and her little friends doubtless shared the scraps of information they gleaned about these practices.

So Ruth grew up a pagan, in a land cursed by the foulness and ferocity of its gods. While growing up, Ruth would have been just as haunted by the rumored stories of what went on in the temple as by the hair-raising screams that came at times from the idol of Chemosh.

This is the woman around whom the story in the book of Ruth revolves. The account tells how Ruth came to know the living God of Israel and how she entered the family of God through a redemptive act of a kinsman-redeemer.

When we first meet her, Ruth is spiritually lost. According to the decree of the Mosaic law, no Moabite could have any part in the worship of the true and living God of Israel until his tenth generation. Translated into practical terms, that meant that Ruth could not be saved, her son could not be saved, her grandson could not be saved, and so on for ten generations. She was not only lost; she was hopelessly lost. Between her and any hope of salvation stood the entire weight of the law of Sinai. The law, with its implacable decrees and unbending demands, mandated against her. There was no way she could escape those edicts that had thundered forth from Sinai.

The book of Ruth, however, shows how God devised a means whereby "his banished be not expelled from him" (2 Samuel 14:14). It tells how a stranger to the commonwealth of Israel, dwelling far away in pagan darkness, was brought into a covenantal relationship with Israel's God. It tells how God not only adopted Ruth into the royal family of Judah, into the outworking of His glorious grace, but also put her in a direct line to David and Christ.

If any book in the Bible demonstrates God's matchless grace and illustrates the divine plan of redemption, it is the book of Ruth. In the Bible, redemption is set forth in two ways: redemption by power, and redemption by purchase. Ruth's story illustrates redemption by purchase.

We can divide the story of Ruth into two parts.

I. RUTH AND THE SOVEREIGNTY OF GOD

Long before Ruth knew anything about God, God knew everything about her: her name; where she lived; her marriage; the name of her husband Mahlon; and her secret thoughts. Long before Ruth knew anything about Him, God set in motion a series of events designed to bring her face to face with Boaz, the man who became her kinsman-redeemer. Boaz did for her in a beautiful, picture-book, Old-Testament-kind-of-way just what Jesus—our kinsman-redeemer—now does for us in a spiritual, eternal, New-Testament-kind-of-way.

A. Drought - A Famine

"It came to pass," we read in Ruth 1:1, "that there was a famine in the land." Thus the first link in the chain that was designed to bring Ruth to Boaz was a sovereign act of God over which she had no control. There was a famine in the foreign country of Judah—one of thirteen famines mentioned in the Bible. Quite possibly Ruth knew nothing about the famine, and if she did she was certainly glad that it was in Judah and not in Moab. The people of Moab would look with smug satisfaction on an outbreak of famine in the country of the Jews, for Moabites had little love for Jews. In any case the famine was far away and seemed unconnected to Ruth's life in Moab. She had no idea that the famine had any relevance to her.

It is like that with our redemption too. Long before we know Him, God works to initiate a chain of circumstances that in the end will bring us face to face with Christ. Often God arranges the circumstances even before we are born. When I think back on my own life, I can see that God was at work before I ever knew Him. This happened; that happened. At the time it never occurred to me that these unfolding circumstances had anything to do with my coming to Christ. But now, looking back, I can easily see God's hand.

B. Discovery - A Family

One day a family moved into Ruth's life, a family of believers. Ruth had never before met anyone quite like Elimelech, his wife Naomi, and their two sons. She became friendly with the family, especially with one of the sons.

We can well imagine that at first Elimelech and Naomi did not like the idea of their older son becoming involved with a Moabite woman. We can imagine Ruth asking, "Why don't they like me, Mahlon?"

Probably he replied, "Oh, they like you well enough, Ruth. The problem is their religion. They have no use for your religion. They think it's a false religion. They're afraid I might become involved in your religion if I marry you." But he married her anyway.

As time passed, Ruth became well acquainted with this family. At the supper table she heard many talks about the things of God, for though Elimelech was a backslider, he was still a believer. Things that Ruth would do, he would not do; places where she would go, he would not go. As for the demon gods of her people, he left her no doubt as to what he thought of them.

She doubtless asked questions about the God of the Hebrews, and Elimelech and Naomi told her about Abraham, Isaac, and Jacob. They told her the wonderful story of Joseph. They talked to her about the exodus, about Moses, and about the Passover lamb. They recounted for her the wilderness wanderings of the Hebrews. Ruth learned how Balak—king of Moab—had hired Balaam to come from the Euphrates to curse the Hebrew people and how, having failed to curse them, Balaam had taught Balak how to corrupt them. Elimelech and Naomi explained that this was why the law cursed Moab. They told her about Joshua and the conquest of Canaan, and recounted some of the stories of the judges. Then Naomi sang Ruth some of the hymns of her people—the song of Deborah, the song of Moses, or perhaps the noble stanzas of Psalm 90. And Ruth drank it all in.

Ruth discovered a world of truth of which she had never dreamed. She learned about a true and living God, a kind God, a pure and holy God, a God wholly unlike the dreadful, lustful, and savage gods of her people. This discovery thrilled her soul. A great longing sprang up in her heart to know more about Him, and she never tired of asking questions. She was not yet ready to make a commitment to this God, but He attracted her just the same.

C. Death - A Funeral

A tragedy happened; death visited that home. There were three funerals, one after the other. Elimelech died. Mahlon died. His brother Chilion, the husband of Orpah (the other Moabite girl), died. We have the sad spectacle of three weeping widows standing around their graves in the land of Moab and mingling their tears.

We can almost picture Ruth standing there, looking down at the remains of her husband and watching as his casket was lowered into the ground. It was all so sad, so seemingly senseless. There was the ache of loss, the mystery of death, and the seeming unfairness of it all.

At this point Ruth could have become very resentful. She could have turned on Naomi and exclaimed, "If this is an example of what your God of love does, don't ever speak to me about Him again. God of love, indeed! Why did He have to take my husband? Why did He have to take yours? Why did He have to take Orpah's?" Ruth could have become bitter, as many people do when death invades a home. But she did not fall into that trap of the devil.

God is too loving to be unkind, too wise to make any mistakes, and too powerful to be thwarted in His plans. The death of Ruth's husband was part of His plan. Mahlon *had* to die because there was no other way Ruth could come to know Boaz as her kinsman-redeemer. In Israel, redemption by means of a kinsman-redeemer meant that Boaz had to marry

Ruth. Obviously he could not marry her if she were still married to Mahlon. So Mahlon's death was part of the overruling sovereignty of God, part of His sovereign grace to Ruth's soul. God planned Mahlon's funeral out of the kindness of His heart.

We can be sure that in later years Ruth looked back to these dark days in Moab. Circumstances had seemed to make no sense at the time, but she could see their meaning now—now that she was married to that mighty prince of the house of Judah and was living in the promised land. She could look back and say, as did Anne Ross Cousin:

> I'll bless the hand that guided,
> I'll bless the heart that planned,
> When throned where glory dwelleth,
> In Immanuel's land.

D. Dismay - A Fear

A crisis came for Ruth when Naomi announced that she was going back to Bethlehem because God had "visited his people." There had been a revival, and Naomi had made up her mind that there was to be no more backsliding in Moab for her. She was going home. She intended to return to the fellowship of God's people.

Ruth must have received this news with considerable dismay because the only light she had was going out. It was not much of a light, the somewhat garbled testimony of a backslider whose advice at this time was anything but spiritual. In her backslidden condition, Naomi was far more inclined to feed Ruth with doubt and discouragement than to sustain her tentative moves toward God with help and blessing. Indeed, Naomi did all she could to discourage Ruth and Orpah from coming with her.

All Ruth could see was a meaningless future in a Moab she no longer loved. All she knew of God was wrapped up at that moment in Naomi, and now Naomi was going away. Ruth now faced an emptiness even greater than that caused by her husband's death. A dark and dismal future stretched before her—a future dominated by Moabite gods, Moabite goals, and Moabite gloom, and ending in a Moabite grave. Ruth could not stand the thought. So the sovereignty of God brought her to her first great decision.

II. RUTH AND THE SALVATION OF GOD

Ruth and Orpah both made the same decision. They would go with Naomi.

A. A Roused Soul

Scripture says of Naomi, "Wherefore she went forth out of the place where she was, and her two daughters in law with her; and they went on the way to return unto the land of Judah" (Ruth 1:7). So far so good. It looks as though Ruth and Orpah became converts. When we get to the end of the story, however, we discover that this was not so. Two walked down the aisle, so to speak, but there was only one wedding. Here we need to pause.

It happens thousands of times: under the stress of an overwhelming circumstance, in the heat of a revival, or under the urging of a faithful evangelist, numbers of people come forward, but that does not mean that they are saved. Some may make a profession of faith and take initial steps toward the promised land, but that does not mean that they are saved. All we have in many instances are roused souls, intellectual responses to the gospel, or emotional responses to appeals.

We must not assume at this point that genuine conversion has taken place. The Lord warned about this in His parable of the sower, the seed, and the soil. The apostle warned about this again and again in the five great warning passages of the book of Hebrews. "Let us go on," he said (Hebrews 6:1). Going on is the acid test of whether or not an initial response to Christ is real. Look at what happened next in the book of Ruth, for it is both sobering and instructive.

As they walked along, Naomi began to doubt. She began to think about her reception in Bethlehem when she showed up with two pagan Moabite women, and she began to throw discouragement their way. She urged Ruth and Orpah to return to Moab. There, she said, they would stand a much better chance of getting married again.

We can see that presently Orpah began to lag behind, casting thoughtful glances back toward Moab. Finally she stopped. The other two, having walked on, missed her and turned around to look for her. There she was, far behind, gazing longingly toward Moab. When they came back to her, Orpah made her final decision: "I can't go on," she may have said. "You're right, Mother. My place is in Moab." We can imagine the emotional scene as Orpah kissed Naomi and said a heart-rending. tearful, eternal goodbye. Then Orpah went back to Moab, back to the demon gods of her people, back to her old way of life, and back to a lost eternity. Her name was henceforth blotted out of God's book. Orpah pictures for us all those whose souls have been roused, but who have never really been saved at all.

Most preachers have known people who have come forward, who have started out for Canaan, but who have had second thoughts. Like Orpah they have come to a stop, turned back, and returned to their old lives, their old gods, their old religions, and their old companions. Such people are as lost as pagans, only more so because once they were enlightened. They have tasted of the heavenly gift, have been made partakers of the Holy Spirit's work of conviction, and have tasted of the good Word of God and the powers of the world to come. Yet they have fallen away. By so doing they have shown that, as Peter said to Simon Magus, they have "neither part nor lot in this matter," for their hearts are "not right in the sight of God" (Acts 8:21). Moreover, the Holy Spirit solemnly says that it will be impossible for those people to be renewed to repentance because they have crucified the Son of God afresh and put Him to an open shame. (See Hebrews 6:4-6.) It is a sobering possibility. "Make your calling and election sure," God warns (2 Peter 1:10). "Let us go on," He urges.

So Orpah turned back toward Moab. Slowly she drew away from the other two women. Sadly but resolutely, she set her face toward the city of destruction—with many wistful looks back at her two dear friends standing there, with many pathetic waves of her hand. At last a dip in the road hid her from view and she was gone. Forever! Her soul had been roused; now it was lost.

As for Ruth, she clung to Naomi. Any thought of going back to Moab was distasteful to her. Still doubtful, Naomi said, "Behold, thy sister in law is gone back unto her people, and unto her gods: return thou after thy sister in law" (Ruth 1:15). Ruth replied:

> Intreat me not to leave thee, or to return from following after thee: for whither thou goest, I will go; and where thou lodgest, I will lodge: thy people shall be my people, and thy God my God: Where thou diest, will I die, and there will I be buried: the Lord do so to me, and more also, if ought but death part thee and me (Ruth 1:16-17).

Ruth was a roused soul indeed.

B. A Redeemed Soul

Not every roused soul is a redeemed soul. Many people turn back, their professions of faith unsupported by the evidence of their lives. But let us look at Ruth.

1. Ruth Meeting Boaz

The two widows arrived in Bethlehem and in their poverty took up their abode somewhere in town. We can imagine that one day Ruth said to Naomi, "Mother, we are very poor. I need to get a job."

Naomi answered, "We have social security in our country," and she explained how Ruth could glean in the harvest field behind the reapers. All that she gleaned she could have. The grain would be hers.

So we watch Ruth wend her way through the village in the dawn's early light. We see her standing irresolutely in the harvest fields, wondering which way to turn. We see her choose a portion of the field that belongs to Boaz. What a story this tells us of God's overruling sovereignty still at work to bring this seeking soul to the Savior. Of all the fields that surrounded Bethlehem, she chose the one that God had chosen for her—the field of Boaz.

Then Ruth met Boaz. He spoke to her kindly, welcomed her into his field, provided for her thirst, and gave to her of his bounty. "Then," we read, "she fell on her face and bowed herself to the ground, and said unto him, Why have I found grace in thine eyes, that thou shouldest take knowledge of me, seeing I am a stranger?" (Ruth 2:10) During this meeting with Boaz, she found grace in the eyes of a kinsman-redeemer whom she did not even know. All this long way God had sovereignly directed her steps. At last she was face to face with the one who could redeem her. Her situation changed quickly after that. In Ruth 2 she is in Boaz's field. In Ruth 3 she is at his feet. In Ruth 4 she is in his family!

2. Ruth Marrying Boaz

We can picture the scene after that first day of gleaning when Ruth arrived home with the great pile of grain Boaz had given her. Naomi must have wondered where Ruth had obtained so much. Naomi had seen gleaners many times in her life, but she had never known them to come home with an amount like that. She no doubt thought that Ruth's old Moabite habits had overcome her conscience and that she had been robbing the barn instead of gleaning in the field. We can imagine Naomi asking, "Where did you get all that?"

Then we can hear Ruth eagerly replying, "I met a man today who was so kind to me."

"What is his name?" Naomi may then have asked.

And we hear Ruth say, "I'll never forget his name, Mother. His name is Boaz."

Then the light dawned on Naomi; she saw instantly what the next step should be. "He is a near kinsman," she told Ruth. "He is the one person in the world who can redeem you and put you into the family of God. You must go to him. Put yourself at his feet. Ask him to redeem you. Ask him to marry you. Ask him to make you his own." Ruth made no excuses and immediately did just that.

She might have made all kinds of excuses that people still make for not coming to Christ, the heavenly kinsman-redeemer. She might have said, "I'm not worthy to come." "I'd be embarrassed." "What would people say?" "I think I've done enough." "Maybe, but some other time." But no, she went to Boaz and asked him to make her his own.

The sequel of this story shows that Boaz loved her enough to make her his own—at great cost.

So Orpah remained lost in dark, pagan Moab while Ruth married a prince of the house of Judah, became a joint-heir with her redeemer, and dwelled with him in bliss.

This story of Ruth can be repeated in the life of any lost child of Adam's ruined race who will come, as Ruth came, to the Redeemer.

6
Boaz,
the Mighty Man

Ruth 2:1–4:13

I. HIS RIGHT TO REDEEM
II. HIS RESOLVE TO REDEEM
III. HIS RESOURCES TO REDEEM
   A. Ruth's Person
   B. Ruth's Property

The first chapter of the book of Ruth is a sad chapter, for it contains nothing but backsliding, death, and unhappiness. And the chapter never so much as names Boaz, the mighty kinsman-redeemer. Likewise, any chapters in our life histories that we write without naming our heavenly Boaz are bound to be filled with fear, frustration, folly, and failure. The chapters of life written by unsaved people, who are total strangers to God's grace, are bound to end in ruin. And if they persist in writing such chapters until the last, their lives will end in eternal night.

Boaz is finally introduced in Ruth 2. From then on the emphasis is on him. He is mentioned ten times in chapter 2 and ten more times in chapters 3 and 4, making a total of twenty times. Similarly, once we introduce the Redeemer into the story of a human life, He is bound to become the center of everything.

Notice also that in Revelation 4 there is no mention of the Lamb. There is only a terrible throne wrapped with thundering and lightning. God is portrayed as hard and adamant as a jasper and a sardius stone. His attendants, aflame with glory, herald the holiness of God. All is remote and unapproachable. But once the Lamb is introduced in Revelation 5, He becomes the center of everything. Indeed, we read about the Lamb no less than twenty-eight times thereafter in the book of Revelation. As hymnist Anne Ross Cousin wrote, "The Lamb is all the glory / Of Immanuel's land."

Once Boaz is introduced into the story of Ruth, he dominates it as the royal kinsman, the mighty man of wealth who is able and willing to redeem. He takes poor, alien Ruth and puts her in the family of God.

Boaz possessed the right to redeem, the resolve to redeem, and the resources to redeem.

I. HIS RIGHT TO REDEEM

The role of kinsman-redeemer was not open to everyone. When Ruth first came home from the harvest field of Bethlehem and told Naomi that she had met Boaz, Naomi exclaimed, "Blessed be he of the Lord, who hath not left off his kindness to the living and the dead . . . The man is near of kin unto us" (Ruth 2:20).

According to the Mosaic law, a kinsman had a threefold function, depending on the circumstances. In the case of *manslaughter*, he had to act as the avenger of blood. His task was to see to it that "whoso sheddeth man's blood, by man shall his blood be shed" (Genesis 9:6). Unless the manslayer fled with all speed to the nearest city of refuge, he had no hope of escape.

In the case of *misfortune*, a kinsman had to watch for the forced sale of the impoverished relative's property and purchase it so that it would remain in the family. Eventually the property had to be restored to its rightful owner.

In the case of *marriage*, a kinsman had a responsibility to his brother's wife. If she were left a childless widow, he had to marry her. Children born of this union were to be treated as the brother's children. Sons of such a Levitical marriage inherited the property of the one who would have been their father, had he lived.

So, not everyone could redeem. It had to be a kinsman, and a near kinsman at that. Here we touch on the genius of the gospel. The Lord Jesus entered the human family so that we might enter the heavenly family. He became near of kin to Adam's ruined race so that He might have the right to redeem. The Son of God became the Son of man so that the sons of men might become the sons of God. "Great is the mystery . . ." wrote Paul. "God was manifest in the flesh" (1 Timothy 3:16). The glory of the gospel lies in this magnificent truth: "The man is near of kin unto us."

At this very place—Bethlehem—nearly two thousand years ago, the second person of the godhead entered human life in order to become our next of kin and have the right to redeem us.

This decision was made in a past eternity. When God the Father, Son, and Holy Spirit decided to act in creation, they knew that they would also have to act in redemption. One of them would need to become a man. "Whom shall [we] send, and who will go for us?" was the great question. "Here am I; send me," was the glorious reply of the second person of the godhead.

In the fullness of time, "God sent forth his Son, made of a woman, made under the law" (Galatians 4:4). When the time was ripe the Holy Spirit went to work and fashioned a body in a virgin's womb. The Son said His fond farewells at home up there in the highest Heaven, stepped off the edge of eternity, and entered time. He stooped down, was contracted to the span of a virgin's womb, and was born in Bethlehem.

A handful of people on this planet heard about His birth. A few poor shepherds huddled against the cold of a winter's night heard the angels' tidings as they watched their flocks in the fields of Bethlehem near the Jerusalem highway. Some wise men from the East, a nobleman-carpenter from Nazareth, an aged woman named Anna, and an elderly man named Simeon were aware of what had happened. The second person of the godhead had become near of kin to Adam's ruined race.

So we meet Boaz. He is introduced into the Scripture text as "a mighty man" (Ruth 2:1). There are five Hebrew words for *man*. This one is *ish*, which signifies a great man in contrast to an ordinary man. It is the word used in Scripture when God is spoken of as a man, and when someone is called a man of God. When Eve said, "I have gotten the Man, even Jehovah," she used the word *ish*: "Ish eth Jehovah!" she said.

So Boaz was mighty, a fitting type of Him of whom Eve spoke when she said, "Ish eth Jehovah." The promised man-child, thus heralded by Eve, was not to be Cain. She was terribly mistaken in that, but we must give her credit because she believed that God would keep His word and send that man.

The father of Boaz was Salmon. That is of interest too, because Salmon was a direct descendant of Judah and a nephew of Aaron. So Boaz was a prince of the house of Judah and was also related to priests of the house of Aaron. In Salmon, the lines of prince and priest converged. This then is the uniqueness of Boaz; he was at once both prince and priest by right of birth. He was, therefore, in the image and likeness of Melchizedek (Hebrews 6:20–7:21).

But there is more. Boaz's first recorded words point us directly to the Christ of whom he was a type. "The Lord be with you," he said to the reapers (Ruth 2:4). One of the names for Christ is *Immanuel*, which means "God with us." In other words Boaz, the kinsman-redeemer, made it the first business of every day to remind his people that a true kinsman-redeemer was on the way. "God be with you," he said. In a parallel vein, the Holy Spirit says, "God with us, Immanuel," pointing us to Christ.

So Boaz had the right to redeem. He was near of kin. He was the mirror-image of both the priest-king and the kinsman-redeemer, the One whose coming means that God at last is with us as near of kin.

II. HIS RESOLVE TO REDEEM

It would have been bad news for Ruth if Boaz had not desired to redeem her. That would have been a greater tragedy than having no eligible redeemer at all.

That possibility certainly existed, as we learn from the story of the nearer kinsman. This man also had the right to redeem, but he did not have the resolve. We need to pause here and take a closer look at him. He presents us with a sorry spectacle. This unnamed individual looked at Ruth and decided that he wanted no part of her.

He had the right to redeem and was willing enough, up to a point, to exercise that right. But what he was interested in was the property. He wanted to get his hands on that. When he realized, however, that he could not have the property without the person, he backed off right away, saying, "Lest I mar mine inheritance" (Ruth 4:6).

Salmon had other sons besides Boaz. This "nearer kinsman" must have been one of them. Probably, too, he was a son by a different wife. He did not want to mar his inheritance by marrying a Moabite and putting Moabite blood into his bloodline. He was afraid of the curse of the law. He was afraid too that by contaminating the purity of his bloodline he might render it impossible for one of his sons to be the promised Messiah.

Boaz was not concerned about this threat to the purity of his pedigree. The reason is evident. His father Salmon was one of the two spies Joshua had sent into Jericho to spy out the land. There Salmon had met (and later married) Rahab the harlot, who became the mother of Boaz. So the pedigree of Boaz was already contaminated—or so men thought. Boaz was not concerned about adding Moabite blood to his pedigree; his line already had Canaanite blood in it anyway.

So the "nearer kinsman" backed off, horrified at the prospect of having to marry a woman from Moab. Perish the thought! "I cannot redeem," he said. He had the right but not the resolve. He had no love for Ruth in his heart, only cold calculations of property and pedigree.

A requirement of the Mosaic law should have been applied at this point. The man who had a right to redeem, but refused to do so, was to be brought before the elders. His widowed sister-in-law was then to pull off his shoe, spit in his face, and say, "So shall it be done unto that man that will not build up his brother's house" (Deuteronomy 25:9).

The plucking off of the shoe spoke of his *disinheritance*. When the prodigal son came home, the first thing the father did was put shoes on his son's feet and put him back into the family. Taking off the shoe reduced the man to the status of a disinherited slave. Spitting in his face spoke of his *dishonor*. No greater shame could have been brought on a man than to have a widow publicly spit in his face with the full approval of the community.

In the days of Ruth, this legal requirement of the Mosaic law had been modified in practice. When the nearer kinsman refused to redeem Ruth, he took off his own shoe and handed it to the one who would redeem—a sign that he relinquished all legal right to the property. Even so the action was quite symbolic.

Look at your shoe for a moment. What does it represent? One part of your shoe, the sole, comes in direct contact with the ground. A shoe is all that stands between a man and the world. The other side of the sole feels the full weight of the body, the full weight of the flesh. Removing that shoe symbolically suggests that there is nothing between the world and the flesh in that man's life. In other words, he is vulnerable.

Look again at Boaz. He had the right to redeem and the resolve to redeem. But underneath that resolve was something else—love. There can be no doubt that Boaz had fallen in love with that destitute, Moabite widow. He wanted her for himself just as much as she wanted to be his. Love led him on to make her his wife, in spite of the law's curse on Moab.

And we sing of *our* beloved Redeemer:

> Out of the ivory palaces
> Into a world of woe,
> Only His great eternal love
> Made my Savior go.
> (Henry Barraclough)

Love brought Jesus down from Heaven's heights to tread these scenes of time. Love shone in all His ways. His was the love that many waters could not quench, the love that suffers long and is kind.

Boaz not only had the right to redeem and the resolve to redeem. There were also:

III. HIS RESOURCES TO REDEEM

It is no accident that the first time Boaz is introduced into the story, Scripture describes him as "a mighty man of wealth" (Ruth 2:1). That is because redemption was a costly business. It would have been of small comfort for a man to have had the right and the resolve, but not the resources. Suppose Boaz had been a beggar. That would not have helped Ruth at all. He had to be rich enough to buy the property that had fallen into default and was now in alien hands.

Now think how rich our Lord Jesus was. Paul wrote, "For ye know the grace of our Lord Jesus Christ, that, though he was rich, yet for your sakes he became poor, that ye through his poverty might be rich" (2 Corinthians 8:9).

We know that Jesus was rich, but we have no idea how rich He was. We shall have to wait until we get home to glory before we discover that. In His country they pave the streets with gold, build their walls of jasper, hang their gates of pearl, garnish their foundations with all kinds of precious stones, and build their palaces of ivory. Where He comes from, the streams are of purest crystal. The throne on which He sits is ablaze with the beauty of jasper and sardius stones and bathed in all the colors of the rainbow. The banks of the crystal stream are lined with the magnificent tree of life. So bright is the uncreated light of that world that its inhabitants have no need of the sun to shine by day or of the moon to shine by night. Jesus' ministers are a flame of fire. Ten thousand times ten thousand sons of light hang on His words and rush to do His bidding—to the utmost bounds of the everlasting hills and the remotest edges of the vast empires of space. (Revelation 6, 21–22) Oh yes! He was very rich.

As John W. Peterson's hymn declares:

> He owns the cattle on a thousand hills,
> The wealth in every mine;
> He owns the rivers and the rocks and rills,
> The sun and stars that shine.

We know too that for our sakes "he became poor," but we have no idea how poor Jesus became. We pick up clues here and there throughout the Gospels. He was born into the home of a laboring man. His mother was a Galilean peasant. She descended from David, but the fortunes of David's house had sunk so low by that time that the rightful heir was the wife of a village carpenter.

We can picture the kind of home in which Jesus lived, for travelers in Palestine before the era of modernization have described such dwelling places. Most likely the living room was located over a cave and contained no furniture. Mary might have been seen there sifting grain through a sieve. In the corner were matting beds that family members rolled up and tucked away out of sight during the day. A few waterpots and jars stood in another corner. The living room was probably separated from the animals' quarters by a pole and some sacking. The noise and smell of the animals were ever present. Outside was a bakestone for making pita bread. The down-stairs cave was the carpenter's shop. The whole situation added up to poverty beyond anything most of us have experienced.

Oh yes, Jesus knew what it was like to be poor. He could say, "The foxes have holes, and the birds of the air have nests; but the Son of man hath not where to lay his head" (Matthew 8:20). To teach the multitudes, He had to borrow a boat. To feed them, He had to borrow a little lad's lunch. To confound His critics, He had to borrow a penny. To ride into Jerusalem, He had to borrow a donkey. To keep the last Passover, He had to borrow a room. He died on another man's cross, and He was buried in another man's tomb. All He had left, when soldiers cast dice for His few bits and pieces of worldly wealth, were the clothes He had on His back. We know that He became poor.

We also know that, because of Him, we will be rich! We are given some idea of *how* rich we will be by the fact that the *earnest*—the down payment of our inheritance, the sign that God is in earnest and means business about our redemption— is the Holy Spirit in our hearts. The Holy Spirit is the one member of the godhead who permanently abides in us and operates through us. Another indication of how rich we will be lies in the fact that as Christians we are now children of God and joint-heirs with Jesus Christ. God intends to dissolve the entire universe, which sin has so sadly marred and stained. Then He will put forth His creative genius and create a new heaven and a new earth that will be filled with wonders and delights beyond anything we can begin to imagine. Jesus Christ has been appointed heir of all things, and we are joint-heirs with Him.

But let us come back to Boaz and Ruth. He had the right, the resolve, and the resources to redeem her. And he did. First he redeemed:

A. Ruth's Person

Boaz bought Ruth. He began by meeting all the demands of the law. That was absolutely fundamental. He could not say, "I love you. I want you. You love me. You want me. So that's all that is necessary." He said, "The law of God has its righteous claims; these must be met. The law legislates against you as a Moabite and raises a barrier between you and God. There is no way that you, as a Moabite, can fulfill the law's demands. But I can, and I will." That is what he did. He set out, methodically and meticulously, to meet every demand of the law. The law of the kinsman-redeemer was a higher law than the law against a Moabite. So when Boaz paid the price of Ruth's redemption—bought her at great cost—he made her his very own.

But he not only redeemed her person. He also redeemed:

B. Ruth's Property

"Ye are witnesses this day, that I have bought all that was Elimelech's, and all that was Chilion's and Mahlon's, of the hand of Naomi. Moreover Ruth the Moabitess, the wife of Mahlon, have I purchased to be my wife" (Ruth 4:9-10).

We should underline that passage. Boaz would have redeemed poor Orpah too if she had not gone back to Moab.

He paid the price for her too. But she lost everything—her hope of redemption, her inheritance, her very soul—in Moab.

Redemption of our property is as much a part of Calvary as the redemption of our persons. That is why there has to be a millennial reign on this planet. God bought this world at infinite cost. In Heaven John has already seen the title deeds of earth pass into Jesus' capable, nail-pierced hand! (Revelation 4–5) One day Jesus will come back to take possession of the earth and run the world as God has always intended it to be run—as a paradise of beauty and bliss far beyond what any words could describe.

Take one last look at Boaz and Ruth. The purchase price has been paid. He has taken her into his arms and made her his very own. He has so satisfied the law's demands that there is now no barrier between her soul and her savior. Now Christ can be formed through her lineage; she can become one of those rare, special people in the Bible who stand in a direct line to Christ.

So it is with our heavenly Boaz, the Lord Jesus. He points to the life that He lived—a life that met all the demands of the moral law. He points to the death that He died—a death that met all the demands of the ceremonial law. He says, "Come!" And when we come, we can sing:

> Now I belong to Jesus,
> Jesus belongs to me,
> Not for the years of time alone,
> But for eternity.
>
> (Norman J. Clayton)

7
Nicodemus, the Man Born Twice

John 3:1-15; 7:50; 19:39

I. NICODEMUS AND THE CHRIST
  A. His Plan
  B. His Plight
  C. His Plea
    1. Three Sudden Stops
    2. Three Simple Steps
II. NICODEMUS AND THE CROWD
III. NICODEMUS AND THE CROSS

Some scholars think that the Nicodemus who came to Jesus by night was Nicodemus ben Gorion, the brother of Josephus the historian. If so, Nicodemus was one of the three richest men in Jerusalem. If so, he became one of the poorest men too, for his daughter was later seen gathering barley corns for food from under horses' hooves. If so, doubtlessly his poverty resulted from the persecution he suffered after becoming a Christian. If so, Nicodemus is certainly one of the richest men in Heaven today.

We learn three things about him. In the book of John, the only Gospel that mentions Nicodemus, we read about Nicodemus and the *Christ,* about Nicodemus and the *crowd,* and about Nicodemus and the *cross.* The first time John set before us the *conversion* of this man. The second time John told us about the *confession* of this man. The third time John recorded for us the *consecration* of this man.

I. NICODEMUS AND THE CHRIST

Nicodemus was "a man of the Pharisees," which tells us something about his *religion;* and he was "a ruler of the Jews," which tells us something about his *rank.* He was unquestionably very religious.

Normally we equate the Pharisees with hypocrisy because most of them were hypocrites. They acted a religious part on the stage of life. Most of the Pharisees, as the Gospels record, were avowed enemies of Jesus. But Nicodemus was not a hypocrite. He was sincerely religious. He fasted twice a week, tithed his income scrupulously right down to the mint and herbs in his garden, kept holidays as holy days, and knew much of the Bible by heart. He was a religious conservative who espoused traditional teaching of the Scriptures and engaged in private and public prayer.

A. His Plan

Nicodemus had heard about Jesus. Indeed, it would have been difficult in those days for him not to have heard about Jesus. The young preacher from the north had taken Jerusalem by storm—so much so that the Sanhedrin was considering what action to take against Him. Jesus had dared to call down God's wrath on those in the temple courts who were acting as money-changers and merchandisers, selling animals for sacrifice to visiting Jews. He had done even more. He had actually driven them out of the temple and had called it "my Father's house."

The temple was the Sanhedrin's special preserve, and temple concessions were very profitable to certain of its members. But the Sanhedrin was cautious about responding to Jesus because large numbers of people believed that He was a prophet.

So Nicodemus came up with a plan. He would privately meet with Jesus. He would talk with Him man to man, perhaps counsel Him to temper zeal with caution, and try to get Him to see that it would do Him no good to infuriate the establishment (of which Nicodemus was a part).

Nicodemus wasted no time in putting his plan into action. Having arranged for a night visit, he began in a condescending and confident way. "Rabbi," he said, giving Jesus the benefit of the doubt, "we know that thou art a teacher come from God: for no man can do these miracles that thou doest, except God be with him" (John 3:2). So the stage was set for a revolution to take place in Nicodemus's soul. He would learn in a hurry that Jesus was not just a man God had sent. Jesus was a man inhabited by God.[1] And He was not just a rabbi or a teacher. He spoke with authority, not as the scribes spoke. In one sentence, as we will see, Jesus swept away everything on which Nicodemus had been depending for salvation.

B. His Plight

The Lord quickly dismissed all the patronage of this influential, well-disposed, and devoutly religious senator. "Verily, verily, I say unto thee," Jesus said, "Except a man be born again, he cannot see the kingdom of God" (John 3:3).

---

[1]This is true as far as the Lord's humanity is concerned, but obviously an inadequate description when we consider His deity.

Jesus swept away all Nicodemus's scrupulous attention to the ritual requirements of the Mosaic law; all his punctilious observance of religious rules; all his fasting, tithing, and praying; all his almsgiving and good works; all his reliance on circumcision, keeping of the sabbath, and observance of the feasts; all his sacrifices and offerings; all his trust in racial pedigree, attainments, and status as a member of the Sanhedrin. Jesus said, in effect, "What you need, Nicodemus, is to be born again."

Nicodemus was so utterly dead in sins, not the least of which were religious sins, that there was only one remedy—a new birth!

Strange to say, Jesus' revolutionary, radical statement struck a responsive chord in this old man's soul. Nicodemus was already acutely aware that all his religious observances, all his morality, and all his good works and attention to ritual had not stilled the small voice of conscience that told him such practices were not enough. This thoughtful religious leader did not question Jesus' startling challenge. He did not ask, "Why?" He knew why. If *he* was not satisfied with himself, how could he expect God to be satisfied? If he was aware of unconfessed, uncleansed, and unconscionable sin deep, deep within—how much more was God aware of it?

Yes, that was what he needed. He needed to be born again. The most remarkable thing about a newborn baby is that he has no past; he only has a future. So the Lord not only revealed the plight; He gave a hint as to the remedy, and Nicodemus seized it. Instead of asking, "Why?" he asked, *"How?"* "How can a man be born when he is old?" (John 3:4)

The Lord then said, "Except a man be born of water and of the Spirit, he cannot enter into the kingdom of God" (John 3:5).

Doubtlessly that startled Nicodemus too. Indeed, the recent preaching of John the Baptist had shaken the whole land from Dan to Beersheba, including all Jerusalem and Judea. "I indeed baptize with water unto repentance," John cried, "but he that cometh after me . . . shall baptize you with the Holy Ghost" (Matthew 3:11). Note John's reference to water and the Spirit. John had been baptizing thousands of people in the Jordan river. He had been preaching *repentance;* his baptism was one of repentance. To be born of water simply meant repentance. To a man, the Sanhedrin, led by the Pharisees, had rejected John and all that he stood for—especially his baptism of repentance.

Jesus brought Nicodemus back to that teaching. No John, no Jesus. That was the formula. If there were no water, there could be no Spirit. Without repentance, there could be no regeneration.

In effect Jesus said, "What you need, Nicodemus, is to go down to John at the Jordan river—religious man that you are, respectable man that you are, rich man that you are, ruler that you are—and repent and be baptized. When you have received John's baptism after confessing your need of repentance, your heart will be ready to receive the next work of God, the work of the Holy Spirit—*regeneration.* Then you can be born again."

That was strong medicine for Nicodemus. It is strong medicine for every religious person to face the fact that religion will not save him, that only repentance and regeneration can effect the kind of new birth that puts a child of Adam's ruined race into the family of God.

C. His Plea

"How?" Nicodemus asked again. "How can these things be?" (John 3:9) He had studied the Bible since he was a boy. He had been a diligent student of the rabbis. He had absorbed the precepts of the great religious teachers of the age. One of his colleagues was the learned Gamaliel. Yet his studies had all been in vain. His Bible teachers had been blind leaders of the blind. Nicodemus too had become a blind leader of the blind. He was a walking Bible encyclopedia, but he had missed the most important lesson of all—he needed to be born again. Learned scholar that he was, biblically literate as he was in the schools and seminaries of men, Nicodemus confessed to Jesus that he did not know how to be born again. Is there a sadder page than this in all of the Bible? Here was a sincere, studious, and scholarly old man who was as lost as any pagan in spite of having spent his life in religious pursuits.

"How can these things be?" Nicodemus asked. We can thank God for this word *how* because most religious people ask *why* and want to challenge the statement that their personal morality, religious observances, and righteous behavior will not get them into the kingdom of God. Nicodemus's question led to his salvation.

Consider Jesus' reply. (If one wants to know "how," it's all here.) Jesus answered the question in two ways. We must look at the *illustration* Jesus gave right here in John 3, and we must look at the *illumination* Jesus gave back in John 1.

Let's begin with what Jesus said in John 1. "He came unto his own, and his own received him not. But as many as received him, to them gave he power to become the sons of God, even to them that believe on his name: Which were born, not of blood, nor of the will of the flesh, nor of the will of man, but of God" (1:11-13).

We will leave Nicodemus while we consider this statement.

These verses contain the nearest thing we have in the New Testament to a formula, the nearest thing to an equation of salvation. Notice the three *sudden stops* in verse 13 and the three *simple steps* in verse 12.

1. Three Sudden Stops

The following three negatives strike down all man's natural hopes for salvation: "Which were born, not of blood, nor of the will of the flesh, nor of the will of man."

Man's salvation is "not of blood"; that is, it is *not of human descent.* It has nothing to do with *the purity of one's pedigree.* The Jews, of course, thought that salvation had everything to do with blood. They thought that they had an automatic ticket to Heaven just because they were Jews and were "Abraham's seed."

Many people today believe the same thing. They think that they are Christians because they were born in a so-called Christian country or because they were born into Christian homes. Years ago our neighbor attended a church service and heard a message on the subject of being born again. Afterward I asked him, "What did you think of the message? Did you feel any need to be born again?"

His answer was ludicrous, especially from an otherwise intelligent man. "My wife," he said, "is a descendant of John Wesley." (That would be like asking a man if he were married and hearing him say, "I had an aunt once who went to a wedding.")

I replied, "That's interesting. Your wife is a descendant of John Wesley. Well, John Wesley certainly knew what it meant to be born again. He was a preacher for years before experiencing the new birth for himself. But being a descendant of John Wesley is not going to help you very much. I'm a descendant of Noah myself, and that didn't help me."

Being born into a Christian home does not make a person a Christian, any more than being born in a stable would have made him a horse. Our salvation is "not of blood." It is not of human descent. It has nothing to do with the purity of our religious pedigree. Jesus said so.

Then comes another sudden stop: "Nor of the will of the flesh." Salvation is *not of human desire.* It has nothing to do with *the fervor of one's feelings.* Few things in this world arouse the passions of men more than their religious beliefs. They will die for those beliefs; they will massacre and murder people over their religious beliefs. People feel strongly about their religious beliefs, and most people put a great deal of confidence in their feelings. But no amount of wishful thinking or degree of religious ecstasy will put a person into the family of God.

There is one more sudden stop: "Nor of the will of man." Salvation is *not of human design.* It has nothing to do with *the confession of one's creed.* Men have invented all kinds of creeds and a thousand ways to get to Heaven. To be saved, people are urged to do this, that, or the other. They must make this pilgrimage or engage in that fast. They must give to this cause or that one. They must subscribe to this set of rules or to that set. They must undergo this ritual or perform that rite. But the Holy Spirit rules out all such effort. Salvation is not of the will of man.

So God is saying to the religious person, "Stop!" To become a child of God and an heir of Heaven is not a matter of birth, breeding, or behavior. It is not a matter of desiring or doing. Salvation operates on an altogether different principle.

Here we should look at the Lord's illustration in John 3. He reminded Nicodemus of a historic day in Israel's history. The children of Israel, on their way from Egypt to Canaan, were murmuring, grumbling, criticizing, and complaining almost every step of the way. God sent a plague of fiery serpents among them as punishment. A serpent's bite meant certain death, and there was no human remedy. However, in His mercy God provided a way of escape, a means of salvation. Nicodemus knew the story well.

Moses made a serpent of brass and hung it on a pole. (The only way to do that, of course, was to affix a crosspiece to the pole and drape the serpent over the crosspiece and nail the serpent there. Thus the serpent was really nailed to a cross.)

To paraphrase Numbers 21:8-9, God said to the Israelites who had been bitten, "All you have to do is look and live. Look at that cross—and live!"

This remedy makes no sense at all to human reasoning. The scientist would say, "What nonsense. There is no correlation at all between serpent venom and a brass serpent on a pole. There is simply no way that looking at that thing can save anyone."

The psychologist would say, "We must look for the cause of our problem in some inhibition of childhood, some aberration of personality brought about by repressive parents. The thing for us to do is to express ourselves sexually. There is no way that looking at that thing will effect a proper personality adjustment and remove the psychological cause of these painful feelings."

The Christian Scientist would say, "Our problem is simply an error of mortal mind. There is no such thing as pain, and death is not real."

The liberal theologian would say, "There was no such person as Moses, and even if there were, he would not have been able to read and write. So we can discount the whole story as Hebrew mythology. In any case, there could not have been a miraculous cure because all miracles have a rational explanation."

The medical doctor would say, "Serpent venom is a highly complex chemical. We need to develop a serum and immunize the population. It is obvious to medical science that just looking at that serpent on the pole is no antidote to snake venom."

The legalist would say, "We need to get back to the law and do our best to keep it. We can only be saved by our good works."

The religionist would say, "What is needed is to offer a costly sacrifice."

The optimist would say, "I'm related to Moses. I'm sure that is going to help me."

But the solution to the Israelites' problem was "Look and live." That is still God's answer to the venom of sin that courses through our spiritual veins, bringing death in its wake. That serpent, nailed to that cross, pointed to Calvary and to the time when the Lord Jesus, who knew no sin, was to be made sin for us. All we have to do is look and live.

In John 1 there are not only those three sudden stops to consider; there are also:

2. Three Simple Steps

"As many as received him, to them gave he power to become the sons of God, even to them that believe on his name" (John 1:12). There is the formula: believe, receive, become. Of these three action words, two refer to our part in being born again and one refers to God's part in this process. Our part is to believe and receive.

The first thing we must do is to believe—but not just anything. We are to believe on something specific—His name. His name is Jesus! When Scripture tells us to "believe on his name," it simply means that we are to believe on that for which His name stands. His name has a special and significant meaning. When the Lord Jesus was born, the angel said to Joseph, "Thou shalt call his name Jesus: for he shall save his people from their sins" (Matthew 1:21). Therefore, to "believe on his name" means that we acknowledge our sins and need for a Savior. It means that we believe that the Lord Jesus Christ can and will save us from our sins. He is the One whom God has provided to save us from sin's penalty, power, and presence. The Lord Jesus can do this because of the cross. Remember, He told Nicodemus that He would deal with the problem of sin on the cross. He would bear the world's sins in His own body on the tree.

We must also receive. The salvation promise is given to as many as receive Him. We can believe something in our heads without believing it in our hearts; that is, we can give intellectual assent to a truth, yet never allow that truth to change our lives. I can believe that Jesus is *the* Savior yet not be able to say that He is *my* Savior. To make Him ours, we must receive Him.

Suppose someone were to offer you a book. You believe that he is sincere in offering it to you. You believe that the book is valuable, well worth owning, and that it would be a blessing to you. You really believe that the person intends for you to have it. Does that make the book yours? Of course not. You must receive it. The book is not yours until you take it.

Likewise, God offers us Jesus as our only possible Savior from sin, but we must receive Him. We must say words to this effect: "Lord Jesus, I believe You are the One who died to save me from my sin. I take You as my Savior. Thank You for loving me enough to die for me. Now come and live Your life in me."

That is man's part: believe and receive. When we do our part the miracle happens. God does His part. He gives us "power to become the sons of God"! Instantly the miracle of new life takes place in our souls. We are regenerated: born again; born from above; born of God. The Holy Spirit of the living God comes, takes up permanent residence in our lives, and imparts to us the very life of God. That is the way we are born again. Nicodemus asked, "How?" That's how.

II. NICODEMUS AND THE CROWD

The second time we read about Nicodemus, he is with his own crowd—the other members of the Sanhedrin. Everyone has his crowd, and any crowd can be intimidating. The Sanhedrin was a Christ-rejecting crowd. It was a jeering, scoffing crowd.

We see Nicodemus standing up for Christ against that crowd. He was not overly brave about it. He did not say much when they sneered at him and suggested that he was ignorant and out of touch. But at least he put in a favorable word for Jesus. It is always a good sign when a person who has been born again stands up for Christ—even when his old friends become new enemies because of Jesus.

III. NICODEMUS AND THE CROSS

Nicodemus did not really begin living for Jesus until the significance of Calvary dawned on his soul. When he finally saw what the world was like by what it did to Jesus, then he broke with the world once and for all. By means of Christ's crucifixion, Nicodemus was crucified to the world and the world was crucified to him. After Calvary he no longer cared what his crowd thought about his allegiance to Christ. Nicodemus lost all fear of what the world might do. The cross revolutionized his thinking about his evil world—all its values and vanities. He was through with it. He stood up to be counted for Christ, boldly and triumphantly.

He may have said to himself, *I may have been too big a coward to be anything but a secret disciple of the Lord Jesus during His life, but I certainly intend to identify with Him in His death and resurrection. Right now He needs a royal burial. Joseph of Arimathaea has a tomb. I have the treasure. I'll invest the price of a king's ransom in spices and see to it that Jesus' body is wrapped in the rarest ointments and the costliest linens. He may not need the tomb for long, but it will be His for as long as He needs it.*

That type of response is always a good sign of a genuine new birth. When a new believer looks at his world in light of the cross and thereafter dies to that world and lives for Jesus, it is proof enough that he has been born again.

The cross made the difference in Nicodemus's life. We have no evidence that he actually visited the cross, although the likelihood is high. Certainly the implications of the Sanhedrin's dreadful decision must have stabbed his conscience into full wakefulness at last. He knew that he should have taken a bolder stand for Christ years earlier. Now Christ was nailed to a Roman cross, and Nicodemus's cowardice and compromise had given silent consent to the deed.

Well, enough was enough. Nicodemus decided not to

compromise any longer. He sought out his colleague, Joseph of Arimathaea, and bared his soul. The two old men looked at each other, horror-struck at where the fast-paced events of the previous dreadful day had taken the nation. Jesus, the Christ, had been crucified! Well, it was too late now for them to undo whatever damage their silence had done in aiding and abetting Caiaphas and his crowd. We can picture the scene.

"Well, Joseph," Nicodemus might have said, "there's still something we can do. We can give His body an honorable burial."

"I've picked up a rumor," Joseph might have replied, "that our esteemed colleagues of the high priest's party are quite prepared to have the body thrown into Gehinnom."

"Never. Not so long as I have a breath in my body," we can almost hear Nicodemus exclaim. "Aren't you building a tomb here in Jerusalem, off the Damascus road?"

"Indeed I am," Joseph might have said, "and it's His. Moreover, I'm going to the governor the moment this terrible crime consummates in Jesus' death, to beg for the body. I have a feeling that he'll give it to me, if only to spite Caiaphas."

"Yes indeed," we can hear Nicodemus say, "and what's more, my friend, you and I will be fulfilling an ancient prophecy. Remember the words of Isaiah? 'With the rich in his death' (Isaiah 53:9). You supply the tomb, and I'll supply the spices."

And so Nicodemus did. He purchased one hundred pounds of costly aromatic spices with which to embalm Jesus' body.

It was the cross that did it. What happened at Calvary opened the eyes of Nicodemus, took away his fear of his fellows and put the cross between himself and the world. Had he known the deathless words of Isaac Watts, Nicodemus might well have said:

> When I survey the wondrous cross
> On which the Prince of glory died,

My richest gain I count but loss,
And pour contempt on all my pride.

Were the whole realm of nature mine,
That were a present far too small:
Love so amazing, so divine,
Demands my soul, my life, my all.

8
Peter
in the Spotlight

John 1:40-42; 6:16-21; Matthew 16:13-25;
John 18:15-27; 21:1-22; Acts 2:14-42; 1 Peter; 2 Peter

I. HIS EYE ON THE LORD

II. HIS MIND ON THE STORM

III. HIS FOOT IN HIS MOUTH

IV. HIS TEARS IN HIS EYES

V. HIS BOAT ON THE LAKE

VI. HIS LORD ON THE THRONE

VII. HIS PEN IN HIS HAND

There is a popular program on television called "Candid Camera." The producers of the show hide cameras in all sorts of unexpected places, set up all kinds of unusual situations, and then film people during their unguarded moments.

One of my favorite episodes involved a stevedore union in New York. The muscle-bound, hard-bitten stevedores were called into an office one by one and were told that they had to go to a bird sanctuary and spend their vacation time watching birds. I can still see the incredulous look on one tough stevedore's face as he pointed a gnarled finger at his hairy chest and growled, "Me? Watch boids? Not me!"

Some of the best photographs we take of children (or adults) are snapshots taken during unguarded moments. Such photographs are not posed; they are real-life pictures.

The Bible gives us a number of candid pictures of Simon Peter—impulsive, impolitic, impressionable Peter.

I. HIS EYE ON THE LORD

Peter had a brother, just about the best kind of brother a man like Peter could have had. He had none of Peter's fervor and fire. He was not nearly as flamboyant, impetuous, or outgoing as Peter.

Peter's brother Andrew had become a disciple of John the Baptist. Andrew spent as much time as he could spare from the family business listening to John and learning how to prepare people for the coming of Christ. Doubtless there were many lively discussions at home about John and his prophecies. Peter perhaps was inclined to be skeptical, while Andrew defended his hero. "He knows what he's talking about, Peter, believe me," we can hear Andrew saying. In the end, even bluff and businesslike Peter was impressed. Andrew described the crowds and the converts of John the Baptist. We can be sure he recounted John's confrontation with the authorities and talked about John's character. "He was raised a priest, Peter, but he is far more than a priest. I'll tell you who I think he is. I think he's Elijah, who has come back to prepare the way for the Messiah."

Then one day Andrew would have burst into that Galilean home. "Simon, where are you? I say, Simon, we've found *Him*. We've found the Messiah; we've found the Christ. I've just met Him—Jesus, the Son of God, the Savior of the world, the promised Messiah!" Andrew insisted that Peter come and meet Jesus too. At last Peter went, finally persuaded by his quietly persistent brother. That day Peter put his eye on Jesus, and he rarely took it off Him again. That day Peter changed. Jesus said to him, "Hello there, Simon. I'm going to call you *Peter*. I'm going to call you *a stone*. There is a rock-like quality about you that I can use." That's our first snapshot—Peter with his eye on the Lord.

II. HIS MIND ON THE STORM

It had been an exciting day. Jesus had preached to an enormous crowd. It had seemed to the disciples as though the prayer Jesus had taught them, "Thy kingdom come," was about to be answered. Jesus had crowned the day by feeding five thousand men plus women and children with a little lad's lunch. Peter, who had seen the boy give his five barley loaves and two small fish to Jesus, had himself been given bread and fish in abundance to distribute to the crowds. He had come back again and again for more. The boy's lunch had turned into a banquet with twelve baskets of food left over. Peter had thought it amazing, and the crowd had thought so too. The people were ready, then and there, to crown Jesus king. Far from accepting the proffered crown, however, Jesus had sent the disciples away and then the multitude.

Oh well, Peter might have thought, *I expect He wants to be acclaimed king in Jerusalem, not here in Galilee. Probably that would be better.*

Jesus had told the disciples to get into a boat and row across the lake, where He would meet them later. He would stay behind for a while to pray. We can imagine Peter, halfway across the lake, turning to the others and saying, "I say, you fellows, I don't like the look of those clouds. I think we're in for a storm." They all knew how dangerous a storm could be on that lake.

Sure enough, the winds howled, the waves heaved, and the disciples struggled against what now had become a terrible tempest, bringing with it what seemed to be certain death. Then one of the disciples saw it—a shape walking on the water toward them. They were terrified. It must be a ghost, some uncanny specter from the deep. Peter was petrified.

A loved voice called out above the shriek of the gale: "It is I; be not afraid" (Matthew 14:27).

Impulsively Peter called back, "If it be thou, bid me come unto thee on the water" (Matthew 14:28).

"Come," Jesus challenged (Matthew 14:29). And Peter did. First he probably put one leg over the side, then the other, holding on to James and John. Feeling the waves unexpectedly solid beneath his feet, Peter took a step, and another, and another, keeping his eye on Jesus.

Then the noise of the wind dinned in his ears, and the fearful sight of the waves caught hold of his eye. With his eye now on the storm, Peter began to sink. "Lord, save me," he screamed (Matthew 14:30).

What a picture. What a lesson. We all know what Peter learned that day. He learned that he must never focus his eye on the storm; he must keep his eye on the Lord. All too often we look at the waves and listen to the wind. We focus on our adverse circumstances when we should be looking to Jesus. When we look to Him, all will be well.

III. HIS FOOT IN HIS MOUTH

Peter always seemed to put his foot into his mouth, just like most of us. That of course is what is so downright lovable about him.

In this particular snapshot, we catch Peter in one of his more spectacular mistakes. The Lord asked the disciples, "Whom do men say that I the Son of man am?" (Matthew 16:13) They replied that some people said that He was Jeremiah, some said that He was Elijah, and some thought that He was John the Baptist raised from the dead. One and all, people were likening Jesus to the greatest men in their nation's history. But that would never do. So Jesus asked the disciples, "But whom say ye that I am?" (16:15)

Peter quickly replied, "Thou art the Christ, the Son of the living God" (Matthew 16:16).

"Blessed art thou, Simon Bar-jonah," the Lord responded to Peter's confession of faith, "for flesh and blood hath not revealed it unto thee, but my Father which is in heaven" (Matthew 16:17). Peter's heart swelled with pride, and Satan got hold of him in an instant. Very few of us can absorb large doses of praise.

Jesus at once began to speak to the disciples of His impending betrayal, crucifixion, death, burial, and resurrection. But all Peter heard was that one ominous word *crucified*. He blurted out, "Be it far from Thee, Lord" (Matthew 16:22).

Instantly Jesus replied, "Get thee behind me, Satan: thou art an offence unto me: for thou savourest not the things that be of God, but those that be of men" (Matthew 16:23). Peter had put his foot into his mouth.

We have another snapshot of Peter doing the same thing on the mount of transfiguration. Peter had been taking a little nap. It had been warm, strenuous work to climb up the rugged slopes of mount Hermon. Peter threw himself down with a sigh and, before he knew it, he fell asleep. When he woke up, he rubbed his eyes with astonishment. There were some visitors talking with Jesus on the mountaintop. And what visitors! Peter recognized them instantly as men from the past. They were two giants of the faith—Moses and Elijah—the great representative of the law and the great representative of the prophets. They were talking earnestly with Jesus, and Peter overheard as they spoke to the Lord about His "decease which he should accomplish at Jerusalem" (Luke 9:31).

Peter "rose" to the occasion with magnificent disregard of the proprieties of the situation. Ignoring the fact that nobody was talking to him and that the conversation did not concern him at all, he again put his foot into his mouth. "Lord," he blurted out, "it is good for us to be here. We've never held a meeting like this. Let's settle down a while. Let's set up three tents—one for You, one for Moses, and one for Elijah." What folly. Peter was putting the Lord on a level with mere men. God from Heaven broke up the meeting and told Peter to be quiet. "This is my beloved Son," He said. "Hear ye him" (Matthew 17:5).

IV. HIS TEARS IN HIS EYES

The shadow of the cross was now dark and impenetrable, and the Lord looked sadly at His somber disciples. A prophecy came to His mind, a prophecy of Zechariah that had long slumbered in the womb of time but was now stirring to life and fulfillment: "Smite the shepherd, and the sheep shall be scattered" (Zechariah 13:7). Already Gethsemane was looming up against the night shadows. Jesus said, "All ye shall be offended because of me this night: for it is written, I will smite the shepherd, and the sheep of the flock shall be scattered abroad" (Matthew 26:31).

Peter bristled. "Not me, Lord," he stated in so many words. "Others might be offended, but not me."

"You think so, Peter?" Jesus replied. "Well, listen for the crowing of the cock. Before the cock crows twice, you will deny me thrice."

And that is what happened. Shortly afterwards, as the Jews bullied and beat Jesus, Peter warmed his hands at the world's fire. Three times he denied the Lord, the last time with oaths and curses. Then the cock crowed, and at that very moment Peter intercepted Jesus' look (Luke 22:61). It was not an "I told you so" look, but a look of such love and forgiveness that it broke Peter's heart. Immediately he went outside and wept bitterly. Scripture does not tell us where Peter went, but we might not be far wrong if we suspect that he went to Gethsemane.

Never had Peter experienced a darker night. He was so ashamed, so sorry, so full of repentance and remorse. Had it not been for the Lord's kind and understanding look, Peter might have taken the terrible road that Judas was now taking and gone out and hanged himself.

What was it Jesus had said? "Satan hath desired to have you, that he may sift you as wheat: But I have prayed for thee" (Luke 22:31-32). That prayer of Jesus held Peter on the path of sanity and kept him from suicide during that terrible night, and the days and endless nights that followed, until he met the risen Christ and received full absolution from Jesus' pierced hands.

V. HIS BOAT ON THE LAKE

After the events at Gethsemane and Gabbatha (John 19:13) and Golgotha, Peter thought that he would never lift up his head again. For some time he seemed to be subdued. Perhaps it appeared to him that although Jesus had forgiven him, the other disciples had not. Likewise, we are not nearly so willing to forgive a brother's fall as Jesus is. We hold it against him, color every subsequent action with suspicion, and act as though we have never fallen ourselves.

Gradually, however, Peter's confidence in the Lord came back and along with it his self-reliance. Jesus had said after His resurrection that He would meet Peter and the other disciples in Galilee. So off to Galilee they went. Back at home in the familiar surroundings of his boyhood and business days, Peter soon began to feel like himself again. Time passed, and still Jesus did not come. Peter wandered around, hating this inactivity. He was essentially a doer, not a dreamer like John. Suddenly Peter came to a decision: he would go back into business. Living by faith was all right so far as it went, but now he was fed up with it. He determined to fix up his nets, clean out his boat, see to his lines, and go back to fishing.

We can imagine Peter resolutely setting out from the house for the beach. The other disciples saw what he was doing and followed him down to his boat. "Figuring on doing some fishing, Peter?"

"Yep, I've had enough," we can hear Peter say. "I'm going back into business, starting tonight. You coming?" No doubt there was some heated discussion. Finally, some of them made up their minds.

Doubting Thomas said, "I'm with you, Peter."

Nathanael, a man singularly free from guile, said, "I'm coming too."

James and John, Peter's fishing partners during the old business days, found the temptation too strong as well. "Count us in, Peter." Two others, for some reason not named, also sided with Peter.

So seven out of the remaining eleven disciples went on an expedition that night; but they caught nothing. Going back into business was not such a good idea after all. They were tired and frustrated. Then as the morning broke, they saw someone on the shore. "Cast the net on the right side of the ship," He called out (John 21:6). They did so, with astonishing results. Then John recognized Jesus. "It is the Lord," he said (21:7).

In a moment Peter, the headstrong and impulsive man, jumped over the side of the boat and waded with giant strides toward the shore. Breakfast was ready. Jesus had some fish sizzling on the fire and some bread. Without a word the disciples took their places and ate the welcome meal, glancing sideways at each other and at Peter, waiting for what might come next. Then it came. The Lord singled out Peter, the born leader of men.

"All right, Peter," we can hear Him saying. "Now tell Me, do you love Me more than these? More than these disciples? More than these fish? Do you love Me, Peter?"

We know with what choking hesitation Peter answered his Lord. He did not dare to use the Master's word for love—the all-embracing, all-compelling, all-conquering love that many waters cannot quench, the love that suffers long and is kind. "Lord! You know I am fond of You" was the best Peter could trust himself to say.

"Then feed my sheep, Peter. I called you out of this fishing business years ago. You are to be a shepherd, Peter—a shepherd, not a small-time businessman on this lake. You are to be a shepherd-pastor of My flock."

VI. HIS LORD ON THE THRONE

It was the day of Pentecost. For ten long days the disciples had waited in the upper room, not daring to leave lest they miss the promised coming of the Spirit of God. They had spent the time in preparation and prayer. Then had come the cloven tongues as of fire; the mighty, rushing wind; the promised baptism of the Spirit.

Down the stairs and into the streets the disciples rushed. Crowds came running. And now Peter was preaching—preaching as never in all his days he had thought it possible to preach—with passion, with persuasion, and with power. The Bible leaped to life, burning in his soul, and the crowd was hushed. Boldly, without fear or cultivating favor, Peter charged home to the crowd their guilt. They had crucified the Lord of glory; they had murdered the Messiah. Conviction settled down on hundreds and hundreds of hearts. Three thousand people were saved in a moment, in the twinkling of an eye. There and then, on the city streets, the church that had been born in the upper room expanded into a vast congregation of men and women and boys and girls—people who were ransomed, healed, restored, forgiven.

What a snapshot. If only we could take similar snapshots of the church today!

Here is another snapshot of Peter, taken quite a while later.

VII. HIS PEN IN HIS HAND

It is likely that Peter always regretted his slow start in the great world missions enterprise of the church. Others had taken the early initiatives. Stephen first saw that the days of Jerusalem, Judaism, and Judea were over. The Spirit had moved on. Israel's persistent rebellion and unbelief made judgment inevitable. Besides, the tearing of the veil had rendered the whole temple system obsolete. Most Jewish Christians, including Peter, were unable to see that truth, but Stephen did. It cost him his life.

Then Philip—not Philip the disciple, but Philip the deacon—was the first to take seriously the Lord's commission to evangelize Samaria. Peter only went there after the work was done.

It was Paul, not Peter, who blazed the trail to the regions beyond, who evangelized Galatia, Macedonia, Achaia, Cappadocia, and Bithynia. It was Paul who left a trail of churches in Pisidian Antioch, Iconium, Lystra, Derbe, Philippi, Corinth, and Ephesus. It was Paul who blazed the trail across Roman Asia and on into Europe.

Peter was a latecomer to the work of Gentile evangelism. Eventually he turned eastward, as Paul had turned westward, and settled in Babylon. There we see Peter with his pen in his hand. The storm clouds were gathering now; the climate was changing. Roman power had finally stirred itself in anger and rage against the church. Peter particularly thought of the Christians in Europe who were bearing the brunt of the persecution. He thought of the many people Paul had led to Christ. He thought of the Gentile churches far and wide, now dear to his heart. He thought particularly of Jewish Christians in those churches and took up his pen.

Peter wrote two letters. The first one dealt with troubles from *without*. The other, with the shadow of Peter's death becoming more and more defined, dealt with troubles from *within*. The first letter had to do with a *suffering church*. The second letter had to do with a *seduced church*. By this time persecution from without and apostasy from within were assaulting the church.

We can imagine with what warmth and enthusiasm Peter's letters were received. Peter had an enormous fund of goodwill in the Christian world. He was respected and revered as a disciple who had been with Jesus from the very first. Peter had walked with Him and talked with Him. Peter had heard all His parables and seen all His miracles. Peter had observed Jesus' flawless life and His fearless death. Peter had been present in the upper room and had attended the last Passover and first communion feast. He had been in Gethsemane and at Gabbatha. He knew all about Golgotha. He had been at the grave on the resurrection morning and on the mount of Olives when Jesus had ascended into Heaven. Peter had been in the upper room on the day of Pentecost when the Holy Spirit came and the church was born. Peter had led three thousand people to Christ with a single sermon. Peter had opened the door of the church to the Gentiles.

So he had an enormous fund of goodwill. His very faults and failings were endearing to people. Peter was "the big fisherman," the bluff, hearty, warm, and impulsive companion of Christ.

Peter's letters reveal his intimacy with Jesus. Peter used the same illustrative style—telling stories, painting word pictures—and made scores of allusions to his many months with the Master. People read and remembered Peter's words of encouragement and hope, his challenge to remain firm in the face of the foe, and his urgent pleas against the invasion of heresy and the vileness of apostasy. People cherished and preserved his letters until they found their way into the sacred canon of Holy Writ. Little did Peter think—as a boy in Galilee reading Job, Jeremiah, Moses, and Malachi—that one day his writings would appear as a divinely inspired addition to the Word of God.

9
Peter
in the Spotlight Again

Acts 3:1-16; 8:5-25; 10:1-48; 11:1-18; 9:32-43;
Galatians 2:11-16; 2 Peter 1:12-15

Dear old Peter. We cannot help but love him. We still have Heaven's photograph album open before us. It is crammed with snapshots as well as formal portraits of all kinds of interesting people. We have seen Peter with his eye on the Lord, with his mind on the storm, with his foot in his mouth, with his tears in his eyes, with his boat on the lake, with his Lord on the throne, and with his pen in his hand. Let us look at some more of those candid-camera snapshots of Peter.

I. HIS HAND IN HIS POCKET

It was three o'clock in the afternoon. Peter and John were on their way to the temple to pray. They had been good friends for many years. In the old days they had been business partners. Now they were partners in the gospel. Far from their beloved lake-shore home in the north, they were living now in the great, busy, impersonal city of Jerusalem. It was the city of many boyhood dreams and many grown men's disillusions. Even so, the temple never ceased to fascinate the two friends. Peter could not as yet realize that the temple was obsolete and no longer served any useful function. Habit drew him back to the temple every time the call to prayer resounded through the city. Perhaps that was not such a bad habit after all.

There were various courts in the temple. When Herod the Great had embellished the temple, he had enlarged the outer court. The Jews did not regard this enlarged court as part of the temple's sacred area. Gentiles were allowed to walk around in this court and it was therefore known as "the court of the Gentiles." Steps led out of that public court into the sacred temple area. After ascending these steps, the Jews (only they were allowed to go beyond the court of the Gentiles) came to a barrier known as "the middle wall of partition." On this barrier was a notice warning Gentiles to go no farther.

Nine gates led through this barrier, and the gate Beautiful appears to have been one of them. Once past the barrier, a Jew entered the court of the women where the treasury was located. Women could penetrate only this far into the temple. Jewish laymen might go farther, into the court of Israel, and there they had to stop. Beyond this was the court of the priests, within which stood the temple itself with its holy place and holy of holies.

According to Josephus, public sacrifices were offered

twice a day—in the early morning and "about the ninth hour" (about three o'clock in the afternoon). A service of public prayer accompanied each sacrifice and another service was conducted at sunset.

Thus we see Peter entering the court of the Gentiles, passing through the barrier by way of the gate Beautiful on his way into the court of Israel. Suddenly something he saw pulled him up short. At the gate Beautiful lay someone who was anything but beautiful—a lame man, a beggar. He had been there most of his life. He had been born lame, and now he was more than forty years old. He had become somewhat of a fixture there. Everyone knew him. Day after day his friends laid him at the gates of a powerless religion. The decades came and went, and that religion did nothing for him. Indeed, it could do nothing for him but let him beg.

With a keen eye for a prospective donor, the beggar sized up Peter and John. He could not hope for much, but they were evidently Galileans and perhaps more ready to part with a coin or two than were the Jews of Jerusalem. So he appealed to them for help.

We can see Peter now with his hand in his pocket. The beggar's eyes gleamed with expectation, but the hand came out empty. Then Peter spoke, and his first words dashed the beggar's hopes to the dust: "Silver and gold have I none; but such as I have give I thee." Peter's second statement raised the beggar's hopes as high as Heaven: "In the name of Jesus Christ of Nazareth rise up and walk" (Acts 3:6). What a snapshot. Peter's pocket was empty, but he was willing to give what he had, and he had something worth far more than a pocketful of gold.

II. HIS LIFE ON THE LINE

The lame man's healing and conversion caused a considerable stir in the temple area. People came running to see what had happened. No wonder. The fellow was leaping and jumping and shouting for joy, hanging on to Peter and John, proclaiming them as his benefactors. As the crowd gathered, Peter saw an opportunity to preach, and preach he did. Soon word reached the temple authorities that these Galilean peasants were preaching—and they weren't licensed to preach. How dare they preach—especially in that detested name of Jesus!

Soon Peter and John were arrested, hauled before the Sanhedrin, and told to give an account of themselves. Gone was the cowardly Galilean fisherman who had once been so ready to deny his Lord because of the casual comments of a serving girl. In his place stood a man as brave as a lion and as terrible as an army with banners. Peter wasted no time in telling the rulers of his people that they were guilty of murdering their Messiah. When asked what authority or name he had used to heal the lame man, Peter gladly told them it was the name of Jesus. Peter then boldly added, "Neither is there salvation in any other: for there is none other name under heaven given among men, whereby we must be saved" (Acts 4:12).

The Sanhedrin demanded that Peter and his fellows agree not to speak any more in the name of Jesus. Fearlessly Peter replied, "Whether it be right in the sight of God to hearken unto you more than unto God, judge ye. For we cannot but speak the things which we have seen and heard" (Acts 4:19-20).

Peter put his life on the line. By now the reality of Christ's redemption, resurrection, rapture, and promised return had taken such a hold on Peter's heart that no man or group of men, however powerful, could intimidate him.

III. HIS FINGER IN THE PIE

Since the ascension the twelve had largely ignored the Lord's great commission: "Ye shall be witnesses unto me both in Jerusalem, and in all Judea, and in Samaria, and unto the uttermost part of the earth" (Acts 1:8). That was all very well, but who would want to go to Samaria? Jews had no dealings with Samaritans. A deep-seated hatred of Samaria was born and bred in the breast of every Jew. No self-respecting Jew would go to Samaria. He would take the bypass road and go miles out of his way, rather than go through Samaria.

We can well imagine some of the heated discussions that took place in the upper room when the question of evangelizing Samaria came up.

Peter might have said, "John, you ought to go. You're the youngest. They might take more kindly to a young man."

John could have answered, "Not me."

Matthew may have chimed in, "You ought to go, Peter. You're the leader, after all. You should set the example. You took the limelight on the day of Pentecost. Take it now too."

Peter might have replied, "Not me."

Then Thomas would have had a word, and with a rare touch of sardonic humor he might have said, "I think Simon Zelotes ought to go—Simon the Zealot, Simon the Jewish patriot."

Simon Zelotes might have answered, "Not me."

Peter could have spoken up, "Andrew, you should go. You're good at bringing people to Christ. You and Philip brought those Greeks that time."

Andrew may have replied, "Not me. I have no leading at all along those lines."

So nobody went. Because none of the twelve would go, the Lord sent somebody else, Philip the evangelist. Revival soon broke out in Samaria, and at once Peter wanted a finger in the pie. He headed a two-man delegation to go down, see what was going on, and perhaps add his apostolic blessing. He found that a very good pie indeed was being baked down there in Samaria. It only had one rotten apple, which Peter soon detected and removed. That trip to Samaria turned out to be good for Peter. It helped to rid him of insular prejudice against the Samaritans. Moreover, Peter's endorsement of Philip's mission made the Samaritans full members, without barrier or bias, in the Christian community.

IV. HIS NOSE IN THE AIR

If visiting the Samaritans was distasteful to Peter, visiting the Gentiles was far worse. He certainly had no intention of doing that. He put his nose in the air with a gesture of arrogant, religious superiority and positively refused to have anything to do with such a visit. He drew the line with the Gentiles.

Then came the compelling, heavenly vision and Peter's resolute "Not so, Lord." The Lord instantly overruled Peter's objections and off Peter went to Cesarea, the detested Roman capital of Palestine, to meet a Gentile soldier named Cornelius. By now Peter's nose was not as high in the air, even though he still did not relish the idea of being forced to be hospitable to Gentiles, of entering a Gentile home, or of eating at what he had always considered to be an unclean table. *What if they serve me pork or ham?* he may have thought. *What if they give me bacon and eggs for breakfast?* He knew that any meal in a Gentile house would include meat that had been offered to idols and cooked with the blood still in it. Everything about this mission ran against Peter's Jewish grain.

However, once he met Cornelius and heard of God's dealings with him, all Peter's doubts were swept aside. His racial prejudice, as deep as the sea and as wide as the ages, was gone. The door of the church was flung open to the Gentiles. The Holy Spirit came down, and it was Pentecost all over again. Not many of us can overcome our prejudices as quickly as that.

V. HIS BACK TO THE WALL

Peter eventually returned to Jerusalem from his mission to Gentile Cesarea. What a reception committee awaited him there. The exclusive brethren, who made up a major part of the Jerusalem church, were waiting for him, ready to read him right out of the fellowship for breaking one of their religious taboos. Peter, they believed, had disgraced them. He had visited a forbidden home and fellowshiped with religiously unclean people. They had their case against him well in hand.

Peter, however, had anticipated their reaction and had taken some Jewish witnesses with him on his mission. Now he called on them to substantiate what had happened. In words brief but pointed, he recounted the whole story and confronted his critics with what God had done. "There you are, brethren," he said in effect. "You take up *that* matter with the Lord."

When we, like Peter, have our backs to the wall, it is good to know that we have God on our side.

VI. HIS SHOULDER TO THE WHEEL

It finally dawned on the apostles in Jerusalem, and on Peter in particular, that the Lord had been serious about evangelizing not only Judea and Samaria but the uttermost parts of the earth. After Philip opened up Samaria, Peter finally put his shoulder to the wheel. He became active in the Lord's work beyond the boundaries of Jerusalem.

His first venture was not very ambitious. He went down to Lydda on the coastal plain of Sharon, about a day's journey from Jerusalem. It was not much of an effort, but it was a start and the Lord blessed him for making the move. In Lydda he healed a man sick of the palsy. Then Peter was summoned to nearby Joppa for the funeral of a gracious, generous lady named Dorcas. He raised her from the dead, a truly spectacular miracle.

These encouraging blessings on his widened ministry greatly stiffened Peter's resolve to keep on reaching out to the great world beyond Jerusalem's confining walls. The legalism and narrowness of the Jerusalem church had trammeled him too long. Then the Lord opened the door to the Gentiles (Acts 10) and Peter's horizons were further broadened. As time went on, his travels widened and so did his interest in the mission field. Eventually we find him writing to believers in faraway places, in fields the apostle Paul had pioneered for the gospel: Cappadocia; Pontus; Galatia; Bithynia; and Asia.

It is a great thing when we set our eyes on regions beyond, when we catch the vision of a lost world and "the untold millions still untold." It is a great thing when we put our shoulders to the wheel. Peter never became the flaming evangelist and tireless missionary that Paul became, but at least Peter threw the weight of his influence and personality behind such a man. We can do that too. We cannot all become Hudson Taylors or David Livingstones, but we can all throw our weight behind those people God has called in our generation to make an impact for Him far and wide in this poor, lost world.

VII. HIS FACE IN THE MUD

Revival had broken out among the Gentiles of Antioch, a thriving metropolis in the nearby country of Syria. Barnabas and Saul had labored there and tremendously expanded the work. The news filtered back to Jerusalem where, for the most part, it was merely a matter of passing interest. In the view of the Jerusalem brethren, no work could be as important as their own, and no church of Gentile believers deserved such high regard in the sight of Heaven as a church of Jewish believers in Jerusalem. Antioch! What a place for a revival to break out. Even Peter was not particularly interested at the time.

Then Paul and Barnabas broke all precedent and boldly carried the gospel to "the regions beyond." At last the Holy Spirit made His move toward what Jesus had called "the uttermost part of the earth." He had waited long enough for Peter; from now on the limelight would be on Paul. Peter probably did not care that much; evangelizing Gentiles did not really appeal to him. True, he had opened the door, but he was content to let someone else press through it. Paul was welcome to assume the work of pioneering in Galatia among wild, barbarous tribes and in other outlandish places.

In the meantime, however, Jewish believers had infiltrated the new church at Antioch and had brought with them typically Jewish sectarian views: Gentiles must be circumcised; they must keep the law of Moses; they must be zealous Jewish proselytes as well as Gentile Christians. It was all so much arrogant, high-sounding nonsense, but it made its impact. The Jewish believers seemed to have plenty of Scripture references to back up their views. Besides, something had to be done to keep the Gentile church from swamping the Jewish church, for ever-increasing numbers of Gentiles were already flooding into the church. Soon Jews would be a permanent minority in the church, and that in their minds would be a disaster.

What better way for us to keep the Gentiles in their place, the Jews thought, *than by putting them under the yoke of the law?* Such was the new Judaizing creed, and Peter did nothing to stop it. Perhaps he did not see anything wrong with it.

But Paul certainly did, and so did Barnabas. It was not long before a delegation came from Antioch to Jerusalem, asking that this effort to Judaize the Gentile church be stopped. Couldn't the Jews understand that there was only one church and that in that church there was neither Jew nor Gentile? A heated debate followed. To give Peter his due, he stood up for Paul. Then the Jerusalem church wrote a letter in which they admitted that Gentile emancipation from circumcision, from the sabbath, from the law, and from the traditions of the Jews was of God. Paul doubtlessly thanked Peter heartily for his share in getting this principle acknowledged in Jerusalem.

James, the Lord's brother, by now had assumed a dominant position in the Jerusalem church. James was a bit legalistic. He had agreed to Gentile emancipation from the law, but had insisted that some stipulations be included in the letter: Gentiles must abstain from fornication, from eating blood, and from eating animals killed by strangulation. Peter was intimidated by James.

Peter wanted to see for himself what was happening at Antioch, so he said goodbye to James and off he went. When Peter arrived in Antioch, he was thrilled at what he saw and grew to love the Gentile Christians. They lionized him. This was Peter, who had spent over three years in the company of Jesus. They pressed him for details. He spent many hours in the homes of the generous and hospitable Gentile believers, eating at their tables, sharing personal experiences of Jesus with them. What happy times these were. What a grand church this was! Peter did not miss for a moment the stuffy regulations of the Jerusalem church. He felt marvelously free.

Then a delegation from Jerusalem arrived in Antioch. They were sent by James to see what was going on. At once Peter caved in. All of a sudden the same old Peter emerged who had once shrunk from confessing his Lord before a serving maid. Under the frowns of James' legalistic colleagues—separatist and exclusive brethren—Peter retreated. He withdrew from fellowship with the Gentiles and refused all further invitations to their homes. He no longer ate meat with them. Throughout the Antioch church confusion reigned. The Gentile believers were dismayed. What had they done? Hadn't this issue been settled? Did they not have in the church archives the letter Peter and James had signed?

Then Paul came, filled with righteous indignation. He took Peter aside and gave him a piece of his mind. Paul's eyes flashed, and his eloquence ignited with holy anger, until Peter became more afraid of Paul than he ever had been of James. Besides, Peter knew in his heart that Paul was right and James was wrong.

With that impulsiveness that made him so beloved, Peter apologized, acknowledged that he had been wrong, and did what he could to put things right. To his credit, Peter never held Paul's actions against him. Peter felt that he had deserved Paul's anger. Years later, when writing to churches Paul had founded, Peter could speak of "our beloved brother Paul" (2 Peter 3:15).

VIII. HIS NAME ON THE LIST

We do not know where Peter was living when Nero burned Rome and blamed the Christians. Roman tradition says that Peter was in Rome, but that is doubtful. There is no concrete evidence that Peter ever visited Rome. Indeed Biblical evidence militates against the idea. Be that as it may, Peter's name was on the "persecution list." Nero, a dreadful tyrant in Rome, was disgracing the throne of the caesars as never before. His name has gone down in history as the arch-persecutor of the church and as a type of the antichrist. Nero so terrorized the early church that the idea was circulated that he would come back as the antichrist in the endtimes.

Nero was out to rid the world of Christians, so he had them rounded up and tortured to death. Some were thrown to lions in the arena or wrapped in animal skins and thrown to wild dogs. Some Christians were burned alive. Some were dipped in wax and burned as torches to light the orgies in Nero's palace grounds. We can well imagine that Nero said, "Get Peter. He's the ringleader. I want him dead . . . crucified, do you hear?"

Peter knew that he would be killed. He had escaped from death at the hands of Herod, but he knew that he would not escape from death at the hands of Nero. Jesus had told him years before that he would one day die for Him, and hinted strongly that he would die by crucifixion. Tradition has it that Peter's last request was to be crucified upside down, to make amends for the time he had denied his Lord.

Peter died a hero's death. When at last he drew his final, agonizing, painful breath and his great spirit departed for the courts of bliss, his beloved Lord welcomed him on the other side. "Welcome home, Peter," we can hear our Lord saying. "Come and see the mansion I've prepared for you on Hallelujah Avenue, just across from Victory Square. Well done, Peter! Ah, here's Gabriel. Gabriel, come and greet Peter, My dear friend."

And we can hear Gabriel saying, "Peter. Oh yes, I've met Peter. Do you remember me, Peter? The last time I saw you, you were sound asleep in prison and I opened the prison's doors for you. Welcome home, Peter."

"And now, Peter," we can hear the Savior saying, "Come and meet My Father." So Peter entered into the joy of his Lord.

10
Herod
the Great

Matthew 2:1-20

I. HIS DESCENT
II. HIS DOMINION
III. HIS DILEMMA
IV. HIS DEMAND
V. HIS DECISION
VI. HIS DEATH

He was a monster in human form, a rapacious wild beast wearing the rich robes of a king. A typical afternoon's entertainment for this well-dressed savage was to get drunk with his concubines and invited guests and crucify seven or eight hundred of his subjects on a public platform in the middle of his capital city. Another one of his favorite tricks was to trap his unarmed enemies in a narrow place and send his legionnaires roaring through the doors in full battle dress, armed with shields and short swords, to slaughter the defense-less captives.

One might wonder why the soldiers obeyed. One might also wonder why Himmler's executioners sat on the lips of death pits and mowed down boys and girls, women and old men—naked and starved wretches—by the countless thousands just because they were Jews.

While this vile man's legionnaires hacked away at their butchery and became soaked with blood, the monster himself would stand and watch, licking his lips, clasping his fat hands together in fury, and crying, "Death to them! Death to them all! They have opposed me."

His name was Herod. History, with its frequent myopia, has called him Herod the Great. During his reign Jesus of Nazareth—the Son of God, the Savior of the world—was born.

We will now ponder this evil king's descent, his dominion, his dilemma, his demand, his decision, and his death. We could subtitle this study "What happens when a thoroughly evil and unrepentant man meets Christ."

I. HIS DESCENT

Herod was an Idumean; that is, he came from Edom and was thus a remote descendant of Esau, the twin brother of Jacob. There had been little love lost between the two brothers way back in the beginning, and no love at all existed between the two nations they founded. Almost from the first, the nation of Israel and the nation of Edom were at war. Just as Esau and Jacob fought in the womb before they ever saw the light of day, so the two nations have fought ever since.

It is one of the great ironies of history that when God's Son stepped off His blazing throne of light and condescended to enter human life by way of the virgin's womb, He was greeted by a king of the Jews sprung from the Jewish people's most bitter foe. The great red dragon was waiting with open maw to devour the man-child as soon as He was born.

But we must go back a little way in Hebrew history. Between the last book of the Old Testament and the first book of the New Testament lie four hundred silent years during which God had nothing to say to His ancient people of Israel. He was preparing to speak once and for all through His Son.

During these long centuries, Palestine was the constant pawn in the struggles between Egypt to the south and Syria to the north. Not only was Palestine constantly ravaged by war, but the overlords, particularly the Syrians, sought to impose raw paganism on the people by brute force. As a result, a family of guerrilla fighters arose who not only trounced their mighty neighbor but won a measure of independence for their tortured land. These fighters were known as the Hasmoneans. For a while they governed brilliantly, but their family squabbles and power struggles eventually attracted the attention of Rome. Pompey made short work of the whole family, imposed a high priest of his choosing on Jerusalem, and hauled the rival priest off to Rome to grace a triumphal parade through the forum.

But Jerusalem and Judea were not as easy to control. Their constant uprisings were a headache to Rome. Consequently Rome decided the man to handle the Jews was Herod, the young Idumean. Herod had been born to command. At age fifteen he had fought Jewish rebels in Galilee. He was glamorous, daring, ruthless, and without conscience. His path to the Jewish throne became strewn with thousands upon thousands of Jewish dead. But Herod cared little for Jewish dead. He was an Idumean, and Edomites had always killed Jews. It was a national sport.

So it was that after various intrigues, after changing sides repeatedly to lick the boots of Pompey, Caesar, Mark Anthony, and Augustus—Herod, still in his twenties, was confirmed in his office as "king of the Jews." A proclamation by the senate, a sacrifice on the Capitol, a royal banquet—and Herod was "king of the Jews."

So much then for his rise to power. The Jews, who were about to crown all their other apostasies and iniquities by murdering their Messiah, and who would then at home and abroad ratify their decision by persistently and pugnaciously persecuting the infant church, had now been saddled with an Idumean for a king. It nearly drove them mad. It certainly did not lead them to repentance.

II. HIS DOMINION

Herod's dominion turned out to be terrible. He filled Jerusalem and his domains with foreign troops and councilors; he filled his cities with spies. No man or woman was safe during his reign. One by one he murdered every rival claimant to the throne. He stamped out the Hasmoneans. He murdered his wife's brother, a lad of seventeen summers and the darling of the Jews. He murdered his favorite wife and both her sons. Only five days before his own death, he murdered his son and heir. No wonder Caesar Augustus declared, "I'd sooner be Herod's swine than Herod's son." Herod hacked and hewed his way through life, murdering and slaughtering six to eight thousand of the best people in his realm.

"The army hates your cruelty," a tough old veteran of many of Herod's wars once dared to tell him. "Have a care, my lord. There isn't a private who doesn't side with your sons. And many of the officers openly curse you."

Herod threw the old soldier on the rack and tortured him beyond all power to endure. He screamed out worthless confessions and accused officers of treason to the crown. Still Herod did not spare him. The soldier's body was twisted and turned on the rack, jerked and pulled until his joints came apart and his bones cracked. The accused officers were then haled before Herod. He harangued the mob and turned it loose; they tore the men Herod suspected into pieces while the king danced up and down screaming for their deaths.

Herod's fiendish cruelties affected his brain. After the murder of his favorite wife he ran raving around his palace and pleaded for mercy from the ghosts that haunted him. "I killed the fairest Jewish princess the world has ever known," he would scream. "I am condemned!"

Herod would storm among his female slaves, point to this girl and that girl, and shout, "You are not Mariamne." Then one day, walking along the quays at Cesarea, he saw a girl who reminded him of his murdered love. Obsessed with her regal beauty, he seized her, ignoring that she was a woman of the streets. Later, when struck with a filthy disease, he screamed, "I knew it was Mariamne. She has come back to curse me!" Thereafter a new fire ran through his veins, a fire of madness begotten of the foul infection he had contracted in his besotted state.

The Romans stood back and laughed. Judea was a long, long way from Rome, and the tyrant knew how to butter up Rome. So long as Herod kept discipline among the Jews, Caesar cared little if a few thousand more or less of the hated Hebrews were slain. Besides, any charges against Herod were made against a king of the scarlet before an emperor of the purple, so Augustus always sided with Herod. What did it really matter if the most brilliant Jews were killed? That only made it easier for Rome to rule the world.

Herod rebuilt the temple for the Jews to conciliate his hated subjects and to indulge his passion for building. He spared neither men nor money to make the temple the wonder of the world. A thousand vehicles carried up the stone; ten thousand men slaved night and day. The work went on almost until the time the Romans burned it to the ground. To build Cesarea in honor of Caesar absorbed the revenues of Herod's kingdom for ten whole years, and to rebuild the temple cost him as much again. But Herod cared little about cost. The Jews could simply pay more taxes. Whole armies spent their lives cutting away the edges of rocks so that the diamond-hard stones could be fitted into perfect walls—each stone uneven and projecting in the center but perfectly aligned along the beveled edge. How many such stones? A million? Twenty million? What cared Herod so long as his visions of grandeur were realized? It took two hundred men to move each stone from the quarries great distances away, but each one fitted like a glove into its appointed place. Yet all would be burned down soon after the final overlay of gold was poured.

So the royal maniac drove his people to do his iron will. They detested him because he was an Edomite. They loved their temple, but they loathed its architect. They hated him.

Everywhere Herod left his mark. He built temples to the gods and to the caesar. He built and rebuilt towns. In Jerusalem, newly built theaters and amphitheaters proclaimed his Hellenistic tastes, the mighty fortress of Antonia proclaimed his debt to Rome, and the temple served as a means to pacify the Jews and come to terms with their faith. At the northwest angle of the upper city he built the noblest of palaces in which to live.

Herod's marked contempt for the Jews was always present. He was fully aware that the Jewish law declared, "Thou shalt not make unto thee any graven image, or any likeness of any thing that is in the heaven above, or that is in the earth beneath, or that is in the waters under the earth" (Exodus 20:4). Yet he placed a wooden image of a Roman eagle over the main gate of the temple. Herod knew too that no such image had affronted Jewish sensibilities since the dreadful days of Antiochus Epiphanes. When the Jews tore the eagle down, as Herod knew they would, he had them chopped into pieces. In its place he put a larger eagle and then, in a letter to Augustus, Herod said that he would kill a million Jews to keep the imperial image there.

So the hated Herod reigned over his domain. He was uneducated and ruled by sheer force of will. The longer he ruled, the worse he became. He filled the country with fortresses directed not against a foreign foe but against the people he ruled. He constructed huge buildings in foreign cities. He paved the streets of Antioch with marble blocks— two and a half miles of them, adorned along their length with colonnades—and paid for them with taxes wrung from the detested Jews.

Into this man's kingdom came the Son of God—born of the virgin Mary, born in a cattle shed, cradled in a manger, and bedded down in hay and straw. What an unlikely place for God's Son to be born—a stinking stable attached to a wayside inn. What an unlikely time for Him to be born—when a detested Edomite sat on the throne of His father David and ruled like a wild beast over the lost sheep of the house of Israel. But born Jesus was, during such a period and in such a place.

III. HIS DILEMMA

One day wise men came from the East saying, "Where is he that is born King of the Jews?" (Matthew 2:2) The question must have thrown the palace into pandemonium. If ever a suspicious, bloodthirsty, ruthless tyrant sat on a throne, it was Herod. If ever a man stained the pages of history with innocent blood after the merest hint or vaguest whisper of a rival claimant to his throne, that man was Herod the so-called Great.

These imposing-looking nobles from the East had arrived in Jerusalem riding on magnificent camels, bearing regal gifts, and telling a strange story about a sovereign and a star. The news must have taken Jerusalem by the ears. Herod's servants must have trod about the mad king's palace softly that day, trembling in every limb at each successive screech of rage that issued from the tyrant's lips.

We can hear him as he raged, "Where are they? Fetch them to me. A king of the Jews! I'll teach them who's king of the Jews. Wise men? Fools to come here publishing such tidings. Where are the guards? Ho, guards. Arrest those men. Where's the inquisitor? We'll roast them alive until they speak."

Herod faced the greatest dilemma of his evil life. He was now confronted with the birth of a babe, with the coming of a greater king than Caesar. This newborn king, as Herod well knew, was the rightful claimant to his throne. This baby was the Son of David, the Son of the living God, the Christ, the long-expected Messiah of Israel. This challenge to Herod's sovereignty came from the highest court of all. So Herod had a dilemma: should he crown this One, or curse Him? It was as simple as that.

Jesus' coming into this world has altered everything. He now challenges every man's throne, hammers at the door of every man's castle, and demands everyone's submission. He comes in seeming weakness—but woe to the man or woman who despises His claims. He comes to us. He demands that we instantly submit to His claims. He is our Maker, God's Son, and the Savior of the world. He knocks at our hearts, putting us into the place of decision. Neutral we cannot be. Will we crown Him or crucify Him? That is still the question.

Most people want nothing to do with Jesus. They wish that He had never come into the world, wish He would go away, and wish to have no part in such a choice. But the dilemma is inescapable. Christ has come. We *have* heard about Him. We must decide whether to crown or crucify the Son of God. There is no middle ground.

Herod's wicked life could all have been changed in a moment by his simple acceptance of Christ and submission to His claims. But Herod, like so many others, did not want his life to be changed. He wanted to hang onto life as it was. All he wanted was to get rid of this choice and to treat Christ the same way he treated everyone else who crossed his will.

So his greatest dilemma had come. Would Herod accept the claim of Christ? That would mean abdicating his throne, surrendering his sovereignty, and yielding his will. It would mean a new way of life and a new center. By yielding to Christ's claims, Herod could be saved. His whole life could promote the interests of God's Son. Herod certainly did not want that any more than most people living today do. Not to yield to Christ's claims, however, was to become even more of an open and avowed enemy of God than he had been before and to court the vengeance of eternal fire. To reject Christ would mean to go on living in wickedness and sin until God finally settled accounts.

IV. HIS DEMAND

"When he had gathered all the chief priests and scribes of the people together, he demanded of them where Christ should be born" (Matthew 2:4). Herod did not know the Bible. He detested the Bible and made fun of it. During this crisis, however, he tacitly confessed that the Bible was the Word of God and that it contained prophecies of great personal relevance.

After World War II when for a brief time Sir Winston Churchill was back in office as prime minister of England, he became troubled by events on the international scene. He remembered Yalta, that fateful conference in February 1945 when he, Stalin, and Roosevelt had met to decide the wartime fate of Europe. Churchill remembered how Stalin had insisted on a second front and had urged Roosevelt to open it soon to take the pressure off Russia. Churchill remembered Roosevelt's plans for opening a second front across the English channel on the shores of France, remembered the gleam in Stalin's eye as he heartily endorsed the plan, and remembered the flattery of that wicked old fox.

Churchill remembered too how he had promoted a different plan. The Allies were already in Europe, fighting their way up the long boot of Italy. He urged that the western powers beat the Russians into the Balkans and into Germany, so that these countries might be truly set free. He pointed out the folly of allowing Russia to get there first.

Churchill remembered Roosevelt's barely-concealed jealousy and how the American president fell for Stalin's flattery. Churchill remembered how he had been given the cold shoulder and how his superior statecraft had been ignored. He remembered Yalta.

Churchill remembered how events had all happened the way he had feared. Half of Europe was now enslaved again, only this time to a far more terrible foe than Germany had ever been. He saw that the West had won the war and lost the peace. He saw Russia astride the world and gaining new strength every day. And that farsighted old warrior-statesman was troubled.

Where could he find light on the things now happening in the world? Ah, there was the Bible. Didn't it say something about these things? He had never lived by the Bible, but maybe it could help him now. Maybe it could cast light on the shadows that lay across the world. Perhaps it could speak with authority to the fears that troubled his heart. Like Herod of old, Churchill began to look for someone who could chart a course for him through the unfamiliar seas of Holy Writ. An appointment was made for him with a well-taught English Christian, Harold St. John.

After greeting his guest, Churchill said, "Mr. St. John, I am a very busy man. You have half an hour; make the most of it. Tell me what the Bible has to say about Russia, about the problems confronting me in this dangerous postwar world." So Mr. St. John opened to him the Scriptures. At the end of the half hour Churchill called his secretary. "What other engagements do I have today?" he demanded.

"Sir," she answered, "at ten o'clock you have an appointment with the ambassador from India. At ten-thirty the foreign secretary wants to see you concerning affairs in South Africa. At eleven o'clock the chancellor of the exchequer is to see you about the budget. At twelve you are to have lunch with the chief lord of the admiralty. At one o'clock . . ."

Churchill cut in, "Cancel them all. Make any excuse you like. Set up new appointments. Anything! I'm spending the rest of the day with Mr. St. John and on no account do I wish to be disturbed."

At the end of that day, the great statesman looked at the humble Christian gentleman who had given him a view of the

Bible such as he had never had before. Churchill saw before him a poor man who had spent much of his life as a missionary in Argentina. He saw a white-haired man with a merry twinkle in his eye. "Mr. St. John," he said, and there was a surprising note of humility in his voice, "I would give half the world for your knowledge of the Bible."

"Sir," replied the courtly old missionary, "for my knowledge of the Bible I gave all the world."

The story does not record how Churchill used the Biblical information he received from God's servant, but history does record what Herod did with the knowledge he gained from the priests and scribes of Jerusalem. They told him that Christ would be born in Bethlehem. Thus Herod was confronted for the last time with factual knowledge of Christ, with the fact that God's Son had come into the world and that his own life would never again be the same.

V. HIS DECISION

Herod's decision was automatic and instinctive. It seems that he never gave the alternative so much as a passing thought. He categorically, totally, and unequivocally rejected the claims of Christ. Then he gave force to his bitter hatred of God's Son, who had dared to challenge his life, by ordering the coldblooded massacre of the babes of Bethlehem. It says a lot about Herod's wickedness that Josephus and other historians do not even record the deed. Herod had already massacred so many people. What difference did a few hundred more make? But God recorded it; God records everything.

Herod failed to kill Christ, but he would have done so if he could. People who reject Christ today may not be able physically to assault God's Son, but if they continue to reject Him as Savior they record their hearts' intentions just the same. God writes down their decisions in His book against the coming day when He will settle accounts at the great white throne. In His tender love and mercy, God sent His Son into this world. To reject Him is an unpardonable sin. That was Herod's decision; may it not be ours.

VI. HIS DEATH

The Bible scarcely gives Herod's death a footnote, but he died horribly. Gone were his sleek good looks. Once lean, he had become obese. He had lost nearly all his hair. Three of his front teeth had broken off. His legs had become great stumps, nine inches thick at the ankles. He could not eat without great pain. A dreadful sickness had spread throughout his body, attacking parts of his flesh and producing ugly, mortifying wounds. He had sores everywhere. His stomach had become so rotten that the guards had to be changed frequently lest they faint from the stench. He was a man of seventy on whose body had been visited all the crimes of his former years. He was foul beyond imagination. His breath was an abomination.

Even as he groveled on his deathbed in mortal agony, his mind ran to murder. He ordered the death of his fifth son. He also remained obsessed with the hatred of Jews. "When I die, I will see to it that they mourn me," he shouted.

He called for his mercenaries—Africans, Cilicians, Egyptians, Persians—the men who had coldly killed off the leaders of Judaism at his command through the years. He yelled at them in a few jumbled sentences: "Go to every city in Judea, arrest the leading citizens, put them in jail, and guard them well. Feed them luxuriously and let them have all comforts. But on the day I die, kill them—kill them all! Go to every city and village; none is too small." He strode about, hacking and thrusting with his right arm, and then fell back exhausted on his bed. Then he gathered himself together again and screamed, "When I die, the Jews may not mourn me, but by the gods they will mourn!"

Herod died as he had lived, a wicked, ungodly man. Laden down with his sins, he died and went to meet his Maker.

Death marks the end of human sovereignty. Napoleon once said of the hated English, "Britain loses every battle except the last." It sometimes seems, in His dealings with men, that God loses every battle, but He does not lose the last one. In the end He sends the angel of death to put an end to an individual's puny sovereignty. From then on God's will is enforced in judgment forever. We need to ask not only, What will we do with Jesus? but also, What will He do with us?

At the time of His birth Herod chose to reject Jesus. At the same time wise men from the East came and worshiped Him. The great question is, Do we take our stand with Herod or with the wise men?

11
The
Prodigal Son

Luke 15:11-24

I. THE FAR HORIZONS

A. What the Prodigal Figured

B. What the Prodigal Forgot

C. What the Prodigal Found
   1. Fair-weather Friends
   2. Far-reaching Famine

II. THE FATHER'S HOUSE

A. His Decision
   1. His Situation
   2. His Sin

B. His Discovery
   1. A Gracious Father
   2. A Glorious Feast
   3. A Great Forgiveness

What is the finest short story ever told? Should we search the works of Rudyard Kipling, Jack London, or Edgar Allan Poe? The finest short story ever told was written nearly two thousand years ago. It is the story of the prodigal son. Not counting the appendix that deals with his older brother, the story of the prodigal is all told in fewer than 350 words. Yet this story never grows old, never fails to charm, and never ceases to hammer home the greatness of our God.

This story is one of Jesus' deathless parables. Every one of His parables is a miracle in words. Every parable is an earthly story with a heavenly meaning; each is a matchless, priceless pearl of wisdom. The story of the prodigal son is essentially the story of a father's love.

Jesus came to teach us a new name for God. God had often revealed Himself in the Old Testament by means of His names. He was *Elohim, Jehovah, Adonai, El Elyon,* and *El Shaddai.* He was *Jehovah Jireh, Jehovah Shalom,* and *Jehovah Nissi.* He was the great I AM. He was the Creator, God Almighty, the Lord who provides, the Lord who is our peace, and the Lord who is our banner. The ages rolled by, and God lived up to the names by which He had progressively revealed Himself. Then Jesus came. He taught men a new name for God. He taught them that God is *Father*—and nowhere more so than in the story of the prodigal son. This story, together with the companion story of the older brother, is simply the story of God as Father. Jesus speaks of God the Father twelve times in twenty-two short verses. If we miss God the Father, we miss the whole point of the parable.

Yet this parable is not without its detractors. Some carping critics have found fault with this, the sweetest story ever told, along two lines. They say first of all that there is no element of *search* in the parable. The father did not run after his wayward boy. He did not scour the brothels, the bars, and the bawdy houses of the far-off country. He did not search through the dives and dens of sin. He did not haunt the gambling joints, the pleasure palaces, the back alleys, and the slums of the far country in search of his son.

Critics say too that the parable has no element of *sacrifice.* God does not smile, nod, and lightly forgive. His holiness demands sacrifice. As we read in Hebrews 9:22, "Without shedding of blood is no remission."

As usual, the critics are wrong. There *is* an element of search. When the prodigal son was far, far away, not a day passed that the father's heart did not follow the son into the distant country. The father did not run after his son because that never does any good.

Every day the father searched the horizon for the first sign of the prodigal's return. Not a day passed when the father did not take up his watch on some vantage point and stare with tear-filled eyes down the dusty road that led away from home. We know that because when the prodigal decided to come home, "when he was yet a great way off, the father saw him, and had compassion, and ran, and fell on his neck, and kissed him" (Luke 15:20). Oh yes, the element of search is there. It is not overly emphasized in this story because the search has already been fully treated in the sister story of the lost sheep.

The parable of the prodigal also contains an element of sacrifice. It is astonishing how critics could have missed the fact that the feast was founded on sacrifice. The father said, "Bring hither the fatted calf, and kill it; and let us eat, and be merry" (Luke 15:23). Of course there is an element of sacrifice. Jesus would not overlook that.

The story of the prodigal son revolves around two focal points: *the far horizons* and *the father's house.*

I. THE FAR HORIZONS

How do we measure the distance to the far country? Do we measure it in terms of *miles* or in terms of *morals?* Or do we measure it in terms of both? In the end the prodigal discovered that the far country was distant from the father's house both in terms of miles and morals.

We could measure how far the prodigal traveled in terms of miles if we knew his starting point (Jerusalem or Capernaum or Nazareth) and where he ended up (Antioch or Corinth or Rome). It would be simply a matter of mathematics or geography.

Suppose the prodigal headed north to Cesarea from

Jerusalem. That would be about sixty-five miles. If he then sailed to Myra on the seacoast of the Roman province of Lycia, that would be another five hundred miles. Suppose he changed ships there and headed on to Malta; that would be another nine hundred miles. If he went on from there to Rome, landed where Paul had landed at Puteoli, and headed north up the Appian way, that would be another five hundred miles or so. By that time he would have traveled some two thousand miles from home. In those days, given the terrible road conditions and the even worse sea conditions, that would have been a far country indeed.

It would be possible, then, to calculate how far the prodigal went if we measure the distance in terms of miles— no matter whether he headed north to Antioch, east to Babylon, west to Rome, or south to Egypt. We have no way, however, to measure how far he went in terms of morals.

When he came back from Corinth or Carthage, from Galatia or Gaul, the road had a beginning point and an ending point. But when the prodigal came back from his immoralities and indecencies, from his debaucheries and drunkenness, there is a sense in which part of him remained in the far country. There he left behind unhappy young women whom he had helped to ruin, and addicted young men whom he had helped to destroy with drugs and alcohol. In the far country remained men and women who were much worse now than they had been before the prodigal had come their way.

In that far country, mothers wept because this young man had come their way with his good looks and daredevil ways, with his fine clothes and bulging wallet. These mothers cried their hearts out because he had swept their daughters off their feet, seduced them, and then laughingly gone on his way, leaving them forever soiled and shamed. In that far country fathers were bowed and bent because this young man had met their sons and taught them how to use drugs and debauch themselves.

So the prodigal had come back, but others had continued

in the wild ways in which he had encouraged them. How far was the far country in terms of morals? His sin was "a rebellion against the entire universe, an anarchy against society, an outrage on everything, a crime against everybody." His sin had contaminated the planet. Even the far country had become worse as a result of the prodigal's pleasures.

We can measure our waywardness if it is only to be measured in terms of miles, but we can never measure our waywardness in terms of example, influence, and cause and effect.

A. What the Prodigal Figured

We can picture this young man, who grew up in that good home, becoming increasingly impatient with his father's devotions, his father's duties, and his father's discipline. The father had lofty principles and high moral standards. He was kindly, but he was firm.

The prodigal decided at last that he had had enough. He was tired of family devotions, tired of the daily tedium of sitting through a reading of the Scriptures, and tired of listening to his father's pious prayers. He was tired of hearing his father say no whenever he wanted to go to this shady place or that questionable house. *If I leave home*, he thought, *I will be free*.

That is always the devil's first lie. "Be free," he says. "Please yourself. Get out from under these restrictions and restraints. Do your own thing." The prodigal followed the devil's lead when he decided he had had about enough of the rules that were part of living at home.

B. What the Prodigal Forgot

The prodigal forgot that the path of sin is expensive. He demanded his share of the family fortune and wasted no time in converting it into cash. Then he packed his bags, lined his purse, and went out—thoughtless young fool that he was—to live on his capital. Of course it soon ran out. Easy come, easy go. The money poured through his wasteful hands. Into taverns he went as the big shot calling for drinks all around. Into gambling joints he went crying, "Increase the stakes." Into fairgrounds he rushed announcing, "Come on, fellows. Everything's on me." The far country was expensive. It took everything and gave nothing.

C. What the Prodigal Found

1. Fair-weather Friends

In the far country the prodigal found fair-weather friends. "When he had spent all . . . he began to be in want" (Luke 15:14). His friends soon left him when he had no more money to throw around.

We can see the prodigal as he looks ruefully at his empty purse and searches his pockets for a forgotten dollar or two. We can see him as he approaches a friend on the street before the news is out that his funds are all gone. "Say, Marcus, could you loan me some money?"

"Sorry, old fellow. Wish I could, you know, but I'm short myself. Why don't you get your old man to send you some more? See you around."

2. Far-reaching Famine

In the far country the prodigal also found far-reaching famine. It was the worst possible time to run out of funds because a famine was on the way. Hard times were coming. Even those who might have been disposed to help him were too occupied with their own needs to care about him. "He began to be in want."

There are thirteen famines in the Bible and they are all significant. This one was providential both in its timing and in its terror. It was "a mighty famine," the Lord says (Luke 15:14), and it came just when the prodigal was most vulnerable. God sends circumstances like this into our lives to drive us to Himself. All too often we forget about Him when things are going well.

Earth's pleasures dried up for the prodigal. His resources failed. There was no more fun, no more food, and no more future. He had come to the end of the line. He had been having so much fun a few months earlier, but now he was stranded in a hostile environment. He had no resources left and no respect left. He had come to the end—but not quite the end. He had to sink lower still before he would give in.

Jesus says that "he went and joined himself to a citizen of that country; and he sent him into his fields to feed swine" (Luke 15:15). Remember, this young man was a Jew. For a Jew to have anything to do with swine was against the Mosaic law, which classified hogs as unclean. No Jew was to contaminate himself with such creatures. Swine-herding was a dirty business in Israel. For this well-bred young Jew to sink so low as to take a job feeding swine was an indication of how low he had sunk and how desperate his need had become. For him to take a filthy job like that then, would be like a man today making a living by peddling pornography.

He "joined himself," Jesus says, to the man who owned this unclean business. The word translated "joined himself" is interesting, for it means "he cleaved to" and comes from a word that means "to glue together." The prodigal found a man who had a job opening, even though it was a detestable kind of job, and he glued himself to this man. The prodigal stuck to him. Surely he could sink no lower.

But he did. "He would fain have filled his belly with the husks that the swine did eat" (Luke 15:16). He sat there by the pig swill. He watched the animals rooting in the garbage. He sank so low that he began to devour the foul food that the pigs were eating. We can see him with a lean and hungry look, his rags and tatters reeking of the swine trough, and his face and hands grimy with filth. We can see him scrape out the bottom of the pig pail and stuff into his mouth the scraps that even the pigs had left behind. He not only engaged in a filthy business; he stuffed himself with the garbage he handled. The prodigal truly had hit bottom. He had discovered that the devil is a cruel master and that the end of the road in this world is a cold place to be.

II. THE FATHER'S HOUSE

As long as the prodigal's money, his friends, and his good times lasted, he did not think at all. He was having too much fun. That is why God allowed him to become friendless and forsaken, homeless and hungry, beggared and abandoned. Now, in extreme need, he began to think.

A. His Decision

1. His Situation

"How many hired servants of my father's have bread enough and to spare, and I perish with hunger!" (Luke 15:17) It was the first kind thought the prodigal had had concerning his father since the seeds of rebellion took root in his soul. His father was good, generous, and gracious. His father would not allow even one of his hired hands to starve to death on his doorstep. *Yet here I am*, he thought, *miles from home, grubbing around in the garbage pails of sin, sitting with swine, trying to stave off my hunger pangs with slops from a pig pail.* He began to feel sorry for himself. *What am I doing here?*

2. His Sin

"I will arise and go to my father, and will say unto him, Father, I have sinned against heaven, and before thee, And am no more worthy to be called thy son: make me as one of thy hired servants" (Luke 15:18-19). That was a giant step forward. There can be no conversion without conviction. Not until the prodigal came to himself could he come to his father.

Not until we see our own desperate need of a heavenly Father's love, compassion, and grace can we make the first move toward home. We must first confess that we are poor, lost sinners. It would have done no good for this young man to return home as rebellious and as riotous in soul as when he left.

We can see the prodigal as he went up to the big house on the hill. The swine were still rooting in the field. The pig trough was almost empty of slops. Holding the pig pail, he banged on the farmhouse door. "Here, Mister," he called, "here's your pig pail. I won't be needing it any longer. I'm going home."

We can see the farmer as he eyed the young man up and down. He looked at the prodigal's tattered finery, his emaciated form, his straggly beard, his unkempt hair, his filthy face, his dirty hands, and his bare, mud-covered feet. He held his nose at the stench of the pigsty that reeked through the ruins of the young man's robes. "You're going home? Looking like that? After what you've done to your father's fine name? If you were my son, I'd turn the dogs on you. That's what I'd do."

"Mister," we can hear the prodigal reply, "I daresay you would. But you don't know my father."

B. His Discovery

The poor young fellow with a new look in his eyes strode out of the gate and headed along the highway for home. He had a long, long way to go. The outward trip had been so easy; it had been all downhill, all fun and frolic. The way back was steep and hard.

His heart must have failed him at times. What if he were too late? What if he had sinned away the day of grace? What if his father, tired of the long wait, had barred and bolted the door?

On and on he went, footsore, weary, and hungry. One fixed hope guided him: his father would be gracious and forgiving. At last the prodigal topped the last rise. There it was on yonder distant hill—the family home. We suspect that at this point his feet must have faltered. He had caught the neighbors' scornful looks as he went past their doors, and he had heard the crowd's caustic comments. Moreover, he had caught a fresh look at himself in the reflecting waters of a pool.

We can see him sit down on a worn stump and put his head in his hands. We can hear him groan in the bitterness of his soul. Coming home had all sounded so easy in the far country, but now . . . He dare not go on.

Then he heard a call; the prodigal heard his name. He lifted up his head and saw an old man running toward him at top speed. It was his father! For "when he was yet a great way off, his father saw him, and had compassion, and ran, and fell on his neck, and kissed him" (Luke 15:20). Yes, his father kissed him. He kissed him despite the filth, the stench, the vermin, the disgrace, and the shame. He kissed him.

"Father," the prodigal said, "I have sinned against heaven, and in thy sight, and am no more worthy to be called thy son" (Luke 15:21).

1. A Gracious Father

The father called for the best robe and a ring. He would not even hear the part about his son being made a hired servant. Likewise, our heavenly Father forgives us. He does not say, "Well, we'll see. We'll put you to work for a while. We'll need some good works out of you before we can receive you back into the family." Salvation is not of works. We come just as we are, wearing all the rags and tatters of our lost estate, and He receives us just as we are. He clothes us and crowns us, gives us the robe and the ring, arrays us with the righteousness of Christ. He gives us a position in the family—a position of love and trust, of sonship and responsibility. We have a gracious Father.

2. A Glorious Feast

"My boy is starving," said his dear father. "Where's the fatted calf?" What a feast there was—what music, what dancing! What a gathering there was in that home to welcome back the prodigal son.

That is just like God. First He saves us, then He satisfies us. Probably the prodigal had not had such a feast since he left home. It was good, wholesome food. It was not the fine, fancy food on which he had squandered his wealth, nor rare, exotic wines of distant lands. It was the good, plain, wholesome food of his father's house. Likewise, God will feed us. He will feed us on His Word and on all the good things that grace can provide.

3. A Great Forgiveness

"*My son*," said the father. "This my son was dead, and is alive again; he was lost, and is found" (Luke 15:24). The son experienced full and free restoration to the family.

Dead, alive, lost, found—in those four words we have the whole story of redeeming, regenerating grace. God is willing to pick up poor, lost sinners who are dead in trespasses and sins, and breathe into their souls eternal life. God will take rebels and reinstate them into His family. All we have to do is come—just as we are.

12
The
Elder Brother

Luke 15:25-32

When Jesus told the parables found in Luke 15, He had a threefold audience in mind. First there were His disciples. They needed teaching; they needed instruction in the truths of God, in the great facts of the faith. To the disciples, these parables were parables of *faith*. The stories of the lost sheep, the lost silver, and the lost sons were intended to instruct the disciples in the great principles and precepts of the Christian faith.

Jesus also had the publicans and sinners in mind. "All the publicans and sinners" were there, Luke said. The statement is a hyperbole. Luke wanted us to know that there were many of them. They were crowding to Christ. To them, these parables were parables of *hope*. These men and women—the outcasts of society, the dregs of humanity, the wretched flotsam and jetsam of the human tide—heard these parables with dawning hope. Although these people were probably outside the pale of Judaism, Jesus loved them. Theirs could be the kingdom of Heaven.

Finally, but perhaps most of all, Jesus had in mind the scribes and Pharisees. They were there too. They were Christ's constant, carping critics. "This man receiveth sinners, and eateth with them," they sneered (Luke 15:2). So Jesus focused these parables on lost ones. To the scribes and Pharisees, these were stories of *love*. God loves lost people. The scribes and Pharisees found this truth hard to understand.

Jesus added an appendix to the last parable. Having told of the wayward prodigal, He painted a portrait of a Pharisee, for that is who the elder brother was. In spirit, in soul, in scorn, and in all his acid sourness, the elder brother was a Pharisee. He was a smug Pharisee, keeping to the letter of the law, and never plunging into open, shameful sin. Yet he was lost. Sin is sin. It is repulsive and hateful to God. He loathes and detests sin for what it is in itself and for what it does in us. Somehow or other, we feel that the foul, filthy sins of the prodigal were almost attractive compared to the sins of the elder brother.

In the elder brother, we have a standing Biblical portrait of people who, while they never stray into the far country, manage to shed a shadow of gloom over everything and everybody. They never go to excess, they commit no crimes, and they violate none of society's laws. Yet they succeed in depressing everyone and in making everyone feel uncomfortable and unhappy. Their sins are not sins of debauchery; they are sins of the disposition. These people are self-righteous, complacent, moody, touchy, spiteful, niggardly, and bad-tempered.

We can picture the two brothers being sent out to play when they were boys. Mother would say, "Now don't play in that stream. And mind you, don't climb those trees. And stay away from the road." The younger brother would always come home soaking wet, having fallen into the stream. Or having fallen out of a tree, he would come home with a torn coat. "Well, I was only bird nesting, Mom," we can hear him saying. "I saw a super nest on one of the branches. It had three little birds in it. And anyway, what about him? He didn't climb the tree, but he threw stones at the birds." The elder brother, on the other hand, never came home with his shoes soaked or with his shirt torn off his back.

Mark Twain captured the spirit of these two boys when he created the characters of Tom Sawyer and Sid. We all like madcap Tom much better than his prim and proper stepbrother Sid. We feel smug when Tom punches the tar out of Sid for some sneaky act of betrayal. But of course the reason is that (as Paul wrote to the Corinthians) we are yet carnal and walk as men.

The parable of this unpleasant elder brother can be broken into parts: his *simple discovery*, his *swift displeasure*, his *surly disposition*, and his *seeming decision*.

I. HIS SIMPLE DISCOVERY

It had been a hard day in the field. The elder brother had been plowing, or weeding, or gathering in a harvest, or herding cattle, or making hay, or picking fruit, or mending fences, or tending sheep. Whatever he was doing, we can be sure that he was doing it conscientiously and competently. Now tired, hot, and bad-tempered, he was coming home for his supper and looking forward to a quiet meal, his easy chair, and an early bedtime.

As he approached the house, however, he heard music and dancing, so he hailed a servant and demanded an explanation. "Thy brother is come; and thy father hath killed the fatted calf, because he hath received him safe and sound" (Luke 15:27).

At that moment the elder brother made a simple discovery. He discovered how much he hated his brother. He hated him for his easy laughter, for his carefree ways, and for leaving him with all the work to do. He hated him for running away from home with half the working capital of the business and for wasting his substance with riotous living. He hated him for dragging the good, respected, family name in the muck and mire, and he hated him most of all for coming back again.

And if the elder brother did not actually hate his father at that moment, he came very close to it. He hated the thought of his father showing any kind of welcome to the prodigal. *The prodigal,* he thought, *should be confined to the servants' hall or, better still, be driven from home. He made his bed, so let him lie on it. It is foolish of my father to make this kind of fuss just because the wretched wastrel has come home.*

The younger son might have gone to the devil in the far country, but the elder brother entertained a thousand devils right in his own heart. There were devils of injured pride, self-love, self-righteousness, bad temper, malicious spite, and all their kin. The elder brother heartily welcomed each and every one of those demons and gave them the full run of his soul as he stood there, stock-still in the field, glowering at the servant who had brought him the news.

II. HIS SINFUL DISPLEASURE

"And," we read, "he was angry, and would not go in" (Luke 15:28). *What?* he was thinking. *Go in there? Go in there and shake that young criminal's hand? Go in there and sit down with him as though nothing has happened? Go in there and sing and dance like a village fool? Not me.*

Harold Begbie spent much of his life investigating amazing spiritual miracles wrought by God in The Salvation Army in the early days when its soldiers marched into the slums of London to seek out the lost. In his book, *Twice Born Men*, he told the stories of the Puncher, Old Born Drunk, the Plumber, and half a dozen more. Wonderful stories they are of prodigal men and women who were won from the far country and brought back to the Father's house. Begbie wrote about similar miracles wrought through The Salvation Army in India. Few books have ever done more to show the contrast between callous Hinduism and compassionate Christianity.

Having delved deeply into stories taken from real life, Begbie turned his hand to writing a novel called *The Vigil*. It is a story of a young minister's spiritual struggle. The minister is earnest about his parish duties, but knows nothing at all about saving grace in his own soul.

The crisis of the story revolves around the death of Dr. Blund, reputed to be the most wicked man in Bartown. This was quite a reputation, for Bartown prided itself on being "the wickedest little hole in England." Dr. Blund spent most of his time drinking gin and playing billiards at the local tavern. The only person who believed in him was his broken, bedraggled wife, whose life had been spent in the shadow of his debaucheries. Halfway through the book, the minister received an urgent call to come to the doctor's bedside. Dr. Blund was dying and needed spiritual help.

The modernistic minister had little patience with the case. He went with utmost reluctance to the doctor's bedside. He could not see why a man who had lived so hideously should be allowed to avert his just punishment in another world by availing himself, in the eleventh hour, of whatever discharges Christianity might offer. In any case, what could he say? If the truth were to be told, the minister was not saved himself. Religion, to him, was just a comfortable profession, the one at which he made his living.

He bent over Dr. Blund and spoke to him professionally of repentance and forgiveness, but the words did not come from his heart and did nothing to comfort the dying man. It did not take the doctor long to see through the minister's facade. "Isn't there something in the Bible about being born again?" Blund asked desperately. "What is it to be born again?" Out of his depth, the minister floundered hopelessly. At last the doctor, to whom each moment was precious, fixed his eye on the wretched vicar. "Tell me," Blund said, "have you been born again?" The minister hung his head in silence. "You don't know," cried the doctor. "You're pretending. You can't help me! You don't know." Covered with confusion and shame, the unconverted minister fled from the room to seek another preacher, one who knew what being born again was all about.

The focus of the story now passed from the soul of the doctor to the soul of the minister. The doctor was saved and passed peacefully into eternity, and to the minister this did not seem fair. *Why should a man who lived so abominably*, he thought, *be absolved of all blame at the last?*

The minister was engaged to a young woman who was born again. "Do you think," he asked her, "that a deathbed repentance atones for a whole life of evil?" Her answer is one of the noblest in all literature. "No," she replied, "but Calvary does!"

> It is not thy tears of repentance nor prayers
> But the blood that atones for the soul;
> On Him then, Who shed it, thou mayest at once
> Thy weight of iniquity roll.
>
> (A. M. Hull)

Now the minister's problem was exactly the same as the elder brother's problem. He was angry and would not go into the house because he could not see, for the life of him, why the prodigal should be pardoned and receive forgiveness so full and so free. This was the reason for the elder brother's sinful displeasure. His trouble was that he knew about *religion*, but he knew nothing about *redemption*. He had a creed, but he did not have the Christ. He had dead works, but he did not have living faith. He knew nothing of Calvary love.

III. HIS SURLY DISPOSITION

The elder brother's sins were all dispositional sins. The Lord Jesus exposed him. Like a surgeon exposing an inner cancer, the great physician opens up to our gaze the meanness and malignancy of this man's soul. The elder brother had not committed a single crime for which society could ever arrest him, but his utter lostness was as real, as terrible, and as Satanic as that of the prodigal in his most abandoned state.

A. His Self-righteousness

"Lo, these many years do I serve thee, neither transgressed I at any time thy commandment" (Luke 15:29). In effect, he said, "I do this, and I do that, and I do the other." This was his religion. His whole religious outlook was one of self-sufficient, moral rectitude.

That is exactly why God cannot take anyone to Heaven on the basis of his imagined good works. In the first place, the elder brother's proud and petulant spirit offset his good works. When God exposes any person's works to the fierce light of His burning holiness, the sins, flaws, and imperfections of those works will be glaring, ugly, and utterly condemning. God *judges* men on the principle of *works*; He *saves* men on the principle of *faith*.

Suppose God were to take people to Heaven on the basis of their good works. They would do just what this elder brother did—begin to boast: "I am here because I did this, because I did that, or because I did the other. I am here because I did not do this, that, or the other. I am thankful that I was not a sinner like other people." Boasting is a manifestation of pride, and pride was the original sin. It was the sin of Lucifer—the morning star, the anointed cherub, the highest archangel of glory. It was pride that inflated him until he was filled with a sense of his own importance. It was pride that changed him from an angel into the devil.

If God were to take people to Heaven on the basis of their good works, moral rectitude, or imagined self-righteousness, they would have to be cast out again for the same reason Lucifer was cast out. The elder brother is proof of this. He took pride in his own imagined goodness. He congratulated himself on how much better he had been than his brother. That attitude kept the elder brother out of his father's house.

B. His Secret Regrets

"Thou never gavest me a kid," he said to his father, "that I might make merry with my friends" (Luke 15:29). The elder brother had the far country in the depths of his heart all the time. In his innermost soul, he was not a bit better than his brother, for both brothers wanted exactly the same thing. The elder brother had also wanted to take the father's resources and spend them on himself, to take all he could and squander it in sinful self-indulgence. The only real difference between the brothers was that the younger brother was more honest. He did not nourish and cherish his lusts secretly in his soul, but had the courage to bring them out into the open.

God knows our secrets. He searches our hearts. He knows where our secret fires burn. He knows the motives that control us, knows "those places where polluted things hold empire o'er the soul."

The elder brother's crowd might not have been the same crowd as that of the prodigal. Their idea of "making merry" might not have been the same as his. The elder brother's crowd probably would not have become drunk. They probably would not have hired women off the streets to share their lusts. They probably would not have caroused, rioted, taken drugs, and brawled. They would have sat around and gossiped, tearing to shreds the characters and reputations of people they disliked. They would have been spiteful, malicious, hateful, and cheap.

C. His Sinful Resentments

"Thou never gavest me a kid," complained the elder son, "that I might make merry with my friends: But as soon as this thy son was come, which hath devoured thy living with harlots, thou hast killed for him the fatted calf" (Luke 15:29-30).

"Thy *brother* is come," said the servant. "This thy *son*," said the elder brother to his father. The brother wanted nothing to do with a fellowship that included such a reprobate as the prodigal. "Thy *brother* was dead, and is alive again," replied the father. The elder brother was totally out of spirit with his father. He was as utterly lost as the prodigal during his worst and wildest days. He lived in his father's house and worked within a stone's throw from it, but he was a million miles away from it in spirit.

This elder brother was moral and religious, but he had nothing in common with his father. Nothing. God's people convene various meetings from time to time so that they can commune with their Father in Heaven. For all his respectability and religion, this elder brother would have participated in none of them.

For instance, we convene the prayer meeting so that we can talk to *the Father* about those of our lost loved ones who are far from God. At the prayer meeting, we plead Calvary love for family members who are away from the fold. The elder brother, on the other hand, never once talked to his father about the lost prodigal. The elder brother knew nothing of Calvary love.

Then too we convene the evangelistic meeting so that we can tell a lost world the news that "Calvary covers it all," that God is a God of infinite grace. At the evangelistic meeting, we tell *others* about Calvary love. The elder brother, however, made no attempt to bring his brother back. He knew nothing of Calvary love.

We also convene the worship meeting so that we can remind *ourselves* of the cost of Calvary love. At this meeting, we think through the nature of Christ's great sacrifice for sin. This meeting is a feast of remembrance, a time when the Father spreads the table for us as a tangible token of His grace. We gather to enjoy His love and tell Him how much we appreciate Him. The elder brother, on the other hand, refused to come to just such a feast. He knew nothing of Calvary love. He had no appreciation of his father or his father's love.

We also convene the ministry meeting so that we can learn more and more about the Father's grace, goodness, government, and glory. There we are exhorted to become more like Him so that we also might radiate Calvary love. The elder brother knew nothing of that love.

We convene the testimony meeting so that we can tell others how we ourselves came to respond to Calvary love. But the elder brother had never responded to his father's love and, of course, had no testimony.

We convene the missionary meeting to commission others to go to the world's remotest boundaries and seek the lost ones to tell them of Calvary love. At the missionary meeting, we pay heed to our Father's heartthrob for a lost and dying world. We each say, "Here am I; send me." The missionary meeting touches our hearts so that those of us who cannot go, can learn to give. As far as the elder brother was concerned, however, the prodigal was in the far country. The elder brother had not the slightest exercise of conscience over his brother's lost condition. He knew nothing of Calvary love.

Instead of participating in these meetings, or at least in what they represent, the elder brother's soul was full of sinful resentments, secret regrets, and self-righteousness. His surly disposition was an ugly reminder that his soul knew nothing of the father's love and grace. His only regret was that he had not had his share of this world's fun.

IV. HIS SEEMING DECISION

A. How He Was Loved

This, perhaps, is the most wonderful part of the parable. The father loved that mean-spirited, self-centered, canting, hypocritical elder brother just as much as he loved the prodigal. "Son," he pleaded, "thou art ever with me, and all that I have is thine" (Luke 15:31). What a picture—the father standing out there in the field, pleading with the elder brother, and urging him to respond to his grace.

B. How He Was Left

We do not know how the story ends. All we know is that at last sight, the elder brother remained outside, still making the wretched choice, still showing that he would rather starve than come inside.

There is nobody too bad for Jesus Christ to save, but some people think that they are too good. The elder brother was just such a person. He saw no need in his soul for his father's grace; he had done no wrong. So he stayed outside—unsaved—but the father still pleaded. In time, however, the father's patience probably was exhausted. Most likely he went inside and shut the door, leaving the elder brother to think malicious, evil thoughts. But Jesus ended the story before it reached that point. This is still the age of grace.

13
Barnabas, a Christian Gentleman

Acts 4:34-37; 9:26-27; 11:20-26; 13:1-13;
15:1-2,36-40

> I. A SINCERE MAN
>
> II. A SYMPATHETIC MAN
>
> III. A SPIRITUAL MAN
>
> IV. A SENSIBLE MAN
>
> V. A SURRENDERED MAN
>
> VI. A SOUND MAN
>
> VII. A SEPARATED MAN

The Holy Spirit says that Barnabas was a good man. That is the clue to his character. The Holy Spirit also says in Romans 5:7, "Scarcely for a righteous man will one die: yet peradventure for a good man some would even dare to die." In other words, Barnabas was the kind of man for whom a person would die. We should carefully note that feature in Barnabas. He was *lovable*. Show me a man that other men would die for, and I'll show you a man well worth following.

Then, too, the Holy Spirit says in Psalm 37:23 that "the steps of a good man are ordered by the Lord." In other words, Barnabas was *leadable*. He was a man well worth following because he was a devoted follower.

With these two clues in hand, let us piece together the story of this lovable, leadable man and note seven of his characteristics.

I. A SINCERE MAN

We first meet Barnabas in the very early days of the church, when it was in the full fire and fervor of its first love for Christ. Barnabas appears at that time in the church's history when men were setting up what G. Campbell Morgan once called "a fanatical communism," governed "not by rule and regulation but by the wild impulse of love." (See Acts 4:34-37.) It was a glorious experiment, and failed, not because the impulse to share was wrong, but because the blazing fires of love died down.

Barnabas, a Levite, had estates on the island of Cyprus. That in itself is of interest because the Levites, in God's Old Testament economy, were not supposed to own land. When God divided up Canaan among the tribes, Levi received no province of his own. Instead, the Levites were scattered throughout the various tribes in the land—some here, some there—to become fulltime workers for the Lord, supported by freewill offerings of the Lord's people in the other tribes.

Barnabas, good man that he was, exemplifies for us the disastrous failure of the Jewish faith. He was a Levite and he owned land. Moreover, he owned it in a foreign country, not in the promised land.

In ancient times Cyprus was famous for its vineyards, wheat fields, oil, and figs. It was a secular Canaan, a land flowing with milk and honey. Anyone who possessed land in Cyprus was rich and influential.

During those early days of the church, many men sold their possessions and put them at the feet of the apostles, but Barnabas outdid them all. He evidently decided that he would become a Levite in deed—a Christian Levite, a landless man dedicated to the social and spiritual good of the church.

He was a sincere man. Such were his great wealth, generosity, noble character, and splendid services to the family of God that the disciples gave him a new name. To his old name *Joseph* they added the new name *Barnabas*, which means "son of consolation, son of exhortation, and son of prophecy." *Barnabas* is a significant name, cut from the same piece of verbal cloth as the name the Lord Jesus used for the Holy Spirit. Jesus called the Holy Spirit the *Paraclete*—"the Comforter, the One called alongside to help." The apostles called Joseph, the Cypriot Levite, *Paraklesis*. His character was such that they identified him with God's Spirit as a comforter and as a man gifted to communicate the Word of God.

This, then, is our introduction to Barnabas. He was a sincere man.

II. A SYMPATHETIC MAN

Barnabas introduced Saul of Tarsus to the apostles. Three years had passed since Saul's conversion. Nobody knew where he had gone. The church had heard rumors that he was saved, but he had vanished. God's saints had thoroughly enjoyed a blessed rest from persecution.

But now Saul was back. Worse yet, he was back in Jerusalem. Worse still, he was seeking to join the fellowship of the church. Naturally, everyone was frightened to death of him. Join the church indeed! Worm out its secrets! Compile lists of its members! Saul of Tarsus was the most dangerous man of the age. Nobody would speak to him. In Jerusalem he was the most hated, most feared, and most friendless man of all. With the blood of so many Christians still red on his hands, it is no wonder that every door in Jerusalem was bolted and barred against him. Christians considered him to be a sinister, Sanhedrin spy.

Against the first rays of that fast-rising sun, Saul of Tarsus, we get our first real glimpse of Barnabas's true stature. Barnabas alone, of all the disciples and apostles in Jerusalem, opened his door to Saul. James the Just—brother of the Lord, chief elder of the Jerusalem church—wanted nothing to do with Saul. Peter, with the keys of the kingdom in his hands, wanted nothing to do with Saul. John the beloved, the apostle of love, wanted nothing to do with Saul. Andrew, who always introduced people to Christ and had a rare gift for seeking out those who needed to know the Savior, wanted nothing to do with Saul. As for doubting Thomas, the scenes in the upper room may have washed all doubts about the deity of Christ out of his skeptical soul; but unless he could have tangible, positive, irrefutable, solid, material proofs of Saul's salvation, Thomas wanted nothing to do with him.

Barnabas, however, opened his door to Saul. He took him in, sat him at his table, and listened to his story. And he believed Saul. We can picture Barnabas taking him around to Peter's place and saying, "Peter, I want you to meet brother Saul." And Peter became so convinced that he entertained Saul in his home for two whole weeks.

What an eventful two weeks that must have been. Perhaps the two men were up early in the morning to pray together and then went to the house of Martha, Mary, and Lazarus. Or they went to Gethsemane. "Here, brother Saul," we can hear Peter saying, "here I fell asleep while Jesus prayed. I can still remember the bloodlike sweat on that matchless brow and the tone of His voice as He said, 'What, could ye not watch with me one hour?' (Matthew 26:40) And here, Saul, right here Judas kissed Him. Here I cut off Malchus's ear. Here the Lord stooped down and picked the ear up, turned it over in His hands, and put it back on again. And here my nerves broke, as did the nerves of us all. We fled like so many frightened sheep, pursued by nothing but our craven fears."

Or perhaps the two men traveled to Gabbatha. "Here, brother Saul, here is where they lit the fire. Here is where three times I denied our Lord. Over there He stood being bullied . . . well, you know the kinds of things they do. I stood here, warming my hands, denying Him, and cursing Him until at last the cock crowed. Then He turned and looked at me, and I went out—back to Gethsemane—to weep like He wept, only in sorrow, shame, remorse, and regret."

Perhaps they traveled up that rugged hill of shame and in silence gazed at the spot where the cross had stood and where the ground had soaked up His blood. Perhaps Peter and Saul went to the tomb of Joseph of Arimathaea, now empty, forsaken, silent, and deserted in its garden of flowers. "And Saul," we can hear Peter saying, "John and I came running, but he outran me. He's younger than I am, you know. But I blundered in first. There lay the graveclothes, just as they had been wrapped around His form. Here, right here, lay the napkin that had been bound about His face."

So Peter woke up early in the morning to give Saul of Tarsus the benefit of his memories. On into the night, beneath the fig tree in Peter's garden, Saul of Tarsus expounded the true meaning of the Jewish Bible as the Holy Spirit had taught it to him during those silent years in Arabia. Doubtless Peter gasped, amazed at this man's gigantic grasp of truth. Only one man—Jesus—had spoken like Saul, who also spoke with authority, and not as the scribes.

The day would come when it would be the greatest honor in thousands of homes across the wide Roman world to entertain the apostle Paul. But Barnabas was the first—the very first man of influence and responsibility—to open his heart and house to Saul. Barnabas was a sympathetic man.

And Barnabas was not the least bit jealous to see Peter making such a fuss over Saul. Barnabas was glad—heartily, humbly glad—that such a pillar of the church would make so much of Saul.

III. A SPIRITUAL MAN

The scene shifts to Antioch. Antioch was wealthy and magnificent, the third greatest city of the world of that time, after Rome and Alexandria. A four-mile-long street ran through the heart of Antioch. It was the home of a Roman prefect and his court. It was a thoroughly Greek city, but also had a large Jewish colony. It was also the seat of idolatry. Here in the world-famous grove of Daphne, heathenism flaunted itself in its most alluring and filthy forms.

Here at Antioch, quite apart from the officialdom of Jerusalem, the Holy Spirit began a new work. Here in sumptuous, voluptuous, sinful Antioch began a wholesale work of evangelism among the Gentiles. This work had no apostolic support or authority, but the preaching of the gospel was an instant success and large numbers of Gentiles were saved.

When reports filtered down to Jerusalem, the apostles decided to investigate this new and startling beginning. The heads of the Jerusalem church chose Barnabas to go and see what was going on. It was a wise choice because Cypriots and Cyrenians were spearheading the work in Antioch, and Barnabas was a Cypriot Jew.

Barnabas was a spiritual man. In connection with his visit to Antioch the Holy Spirit tells us that Barnabas was "a good man, and full of the Holy Ghost and of faith" (Acts 11:24). Because he was spiritual, he did not lecture the new believers. He did not say, "There are no authorized teachers here. No provision has been made for the proper administration of the sacrament."

He did not say, "We need a manual of theology so that these new believers can be systematically trained in sound Christian doctrine."

He did not say, "There is too much emotionalism in this work. This work needs a stronger emphasis on the moral side of the Christian faith, especially in such a vile city as Antioch."

No. Barnabas was spiritual. We read that "when he came, and had seen the grace of God, [he] was glad, and exhorted them all, that with purpose of heart they would cleave unto the Lord . . . and much people was added to the Lord" (Acts 11:23-24). He preached Christ, and the revival fires spread.

IV. A SENSIBLE MAN

It did not take Barnabas long to realize that the work in Antioch was growing so fast that it needed a stronger hand than his to guide it correctly. What should he do? To whom should he turn? Should he go back to Jerusalem and recruit help there? His mind ran down the list of the apostles. *What about Peter? No. Peter is too impulsive. What about James, the Lord's brother? No. He is too rigid. What about Thomas? No. Thomas is too skeptical. What about John? John is too emotional. What about Philip the evangelist? No. He is no longer in Jerusalem; he is in Cesarea and is too busy.* Indeed, Barnabas could not think of anyone in Jerusalem who could guide what was going on at Antioch. *What a pity Stephen is dead. Stephen would have been the man . . . What about Saul of Tarsus?*

"Then departed Barnabas to Tarsus, for to seek Saul: And when he had found him, he brought him unto Antioch" (Acts 11:25-26). It was a bold move. Instead of going to Jerusalem, he went to Tarsus. The word rendered "to seek" suggests that Barnabas did not really know where to find Saul. He went to "hunt him up." He took on himself the risk and immense responsibility of bringing Saul of Tarsus to Antioch without first submitting Saul's name to church authorities in Jerusalem. The Spirit of God led Barnabas to this decision.

Saul and Barnabas worked together in Antioch for at least a year to enlarge the church, to encourage the believers, and to evangelize the city. At Antioch pagans coined the term *Christians* as a nickname of contempt for believers. A sensible man, Barnabas had been absolutely right in his judgment. Saul was indeed the man for the job at Antioch.

Barnabas must have known that by bringing in Saul of Tarsus, he was bringing in a bigger man than he was—bigger in talent and genius, bigger in his grasp of truth, bigger in breadth of vision and boldness of action. But, as Alexander Whyte said, "To have the heart to discover a more talented man than yourself, and then to have the heart to go to Tarsus for him, and to make way for him in Antioch, is far better than to have all Saul's talents to yourself. . . . Speaking for myself," said that fiery Scottish preacher, "I would far rather have a little of Barnabas' grace than have all of Saul's genius."[1] Or, to quote Spurgeon's unforgettable verse:

> It takes more grace than I can tell,
> To play the second fiddle well.

It is rare indeed to find an older man, held high in the opinions of his brethren, who will allow himself to be eclipsed by a younger man. Barnabas was sensible enough to recognize his limitations.

V. A SURRENDERED MAN

"Separate me Barnabas and Saul," said the Holy Spirit to the elders of the Gentile church at Antioch (Acts 13:2). The Holy Spirit had called Barnabas and Saul, their two best men, their two ablest preachers and personal workers. It was the missionary call, the call of God to the regions beyond. It was a mighty mandate from on high, a mandate to reach out now to "the uttermost part of the earth," to take the glad tidings of the gospel to untold millions. Barnabas and Saul had been chosen.

---

[1] *Bible Characters from the Old Testament and the New Testament* (Grand Rapids: Zondervan, 1967), 139.

Barnabas was a surrendered man. He could have said, "I'm needed here. I want to stay here. I like it here. I feel much more suited to this kind of work than to pioneering work on the foreign field. I think I have done my share. Let another, younger man go. I'll stay here and mobilize the church to give, pray, and support others on the front-lines of Galatia and Gaul. What about John Mark? He's willing enough. I'll give him a crash course in evangelism and soul-winning. Paul can take him."

But Barnabas did not say these things. He had surrendered all to God. For months now he had been aware—as he and Paul had pioneered together at Antioch, as they had prayed together about the great, lost Gentile world—that the Spirit of God was burdening him, calling him, and separating him to carry out a work of worldwide evangelism.

Then, when the same Holy Spirit began to exercise the godly elders in the Antioch church regarding the great world of lost people and about sending Barnabas and Saul out as missionaries, that was it. Barnabas, the surrendered man, simply said in effect, "Here am I; send me." We remember the Holy Spirit's assessment of Barnabas: he was a good man, full of the Holy Spirit, and full of faith. These are the three great qualifications for a missionary. Education, zeal, or financial support does not make a missionary. A good man, full of the Holy Spirit, and full of faith—these are the marks of a missionary. These qualifications are what we should look for in missionaries we send forth.

Barnabas's goodness gave him the *compassion* that he needed. He no doubt was touched by the feelings of others' infirmities. He wanted to see other men discover the goodness that is of God.

Barnabas was full of the Holy Spirit. That gave him the *competence* he needed—competence to make a thousand decisions, to deal with spiritual needs, and to know when and where to go.

Barnabas was full of faith. That gave him the *compulsion*

he needed—the willingness to do and dare, the ability to trust God for provision, protection, and progress.

VI. A SOUND MAN

When the Jerusalem church wanted to send a man to Antioch to investigate the new work among the Gentiles, what sounder man could they have found than Barnabas? Now that a crisis had arisen in the Antioch church because of false instruction sponsored by teachers from Jerusalem, now that there was a need to send a man from Antioch to Jerusalem to settle the matter, what sounder man could be found than Barnabas? And so Barnabas (along with Paul and others) was sent.

The issues at stake were enormous. False teachers maintained that Gentile Christians should be circumcised and that unless they were circumcised they could not possibly be saved. That made sense to these legalists. The Christian Jew looked upon his Christianity as the natural outcome of his Judaism. He had come up through circumcision, the law, and the entire ritual and tradition of Judaism to faith in Christ. How could Gentiles be saved by starting halfway?

Apart from Barnabas, Paul would probably have broken with the Jerusalem church and the other apostles altogether and gone off on his own in the interests of truth. That would have permanently divided the church into two parts: a Gentile church and a Jewish (Hebrew Christian) church. The conference to settle the dispute needed a sound man who would mediate between the fiery zeal of the apostle Paul and the false zeal of the legalists. Who could be more conciliatory than Barnabas?

VII. A SEPARATED MAN

The question about the Gentiles and Judaism was settled at the Jerusalem conference. There would not be two churches (a Gentile church and a Hebrew Christian church), but one united church.

The good news was brought back to Antioch. The work flourished, and Peter came up to see it for himself. Then, when certain legalistic Jewish brethren from Jerusalem came to Antioch to persist in teaching their divisive doctrine, Peter—to keep in the good graces of James—went along with them. And, alas, so did Barnabas.

The first crack in an otherwise flawless character surfaced. Barnabas came within sight of being an altogether perfect man. But, after all, he was made of the same clay as ourselves.

Fiery Paul gave Peter the greatest dressing down of his life for his cowardice. It seems, however, that Paul said nothing to Barnabas. On the contrary, shortly afterward, Paul proposed to Barnabas that they set out on a second missionary journey.

Barnabas agreed. But then the separation came; the hairline crack in Barnabas's character split wide open during a lamentable quarrel with Paul over John Mark. Barnabas wanted to take his young nephew along again, despite John Mark's failure on the first missionary journey. Paul, however, adamantly refused even to consider this option.

The Holy Spirit draws our attention to "the contention" between them (Acts 15:39). The Greek word translated *contention* is one of Luke's medical terms. It is the word from which is derived our English word *paroxysm*, which means "fit" or "sudden attack" or "outburst of rage." This was not a small disagreement. Its thunder reverberated throughout the whole church. No doubt people took sides—as they have ever since.

G. Campbell Morgan said, "My own sympathy is entirely with Barnabas."

Alexander Whyte said, "Barnabas' ship strikes the rocks till one of the noblest characters in the New Testament is shattered and all but sunk under our very eyes."[2]

Who, then, was right? Let us consider the arguments that

---

[2]Ibid.

Paul and Barnabas might have offered during their more lucid moments when discussion took the place of dissension.

First listen to Barnabas:

"Mark," he says, "is my nephew, and I feel personally responsible for his spiritual well-being. What a travesty it would be if I, having risked my life for the heathen in foreign fields, had no concern about my own relatives. I admit that Mark failed, that he turned back after putting his hand to the plow. But I could point out many of my own failures too. Can we not at least credit Mark with enthusiasm for the cause of Christ? At least he started on the journey, when thousands of others stayed comfortably at home. And now, fully alive to the perils and pitfalls of the way, he wants to go again. He is thoroughly ashamed of himself and thoroughly repentant of his past disgraceful actions. Can we afford to break this bruised reed and quench this smoking flax? Shall we act in a way that is contrary to the Spirit of the Lord Jesus Christ, who picked up even Peter when—not once, not twice, but three times—he denied his Lord? Yes, indeed, Jesus picked Peter up and gave him an honored place in the forefront of the apostolic band."

Now listen to Paul:

"Barnabas, I must confess that I am deeply moved by all that you have to say. My heart is fully alive to a similar debt I owe you. Were it not for your influence in the face of opposition, perhaps I would not be where I am today. Because Mark is your nephew, I fervently wish that I could bow to your desire. But there are larger considerations than those of family and friendship. The cause and claims of Christ dwarf all lesser relationships.

"Mark might render excellent service to the Lord in other fields. For instance, he has a way with words. Let him write an account of the life of Christ for the blessing of all mankind. But for this particular enterprise—for a mission that calls for a cool head, an iron nerve, a steady hand—Mark is totally unequipped. He deserted the cause right when he was needed the most, right when difficulties and dangers loomed largest.

We cannot afford to run that risk again. To have a missionary play the coward before pagan converts who are faced with the world's bitter hostility would be disastrous. It would put Christ to open shame. It would bring mockery on the mission and the message. People would say that we did not practice what we preached. They would say that we expected them to face perils from which we ourselves shrank.

"I have long ago forgiven Mark, freely and with all my heart. I pray for him and long to see him greatly used of God. He has a gentle spirit. Everyone loves him for his sincerity, for his sweetness of disposition, and for his willingness to work for God. It would not be fair to Mark to expose him to situations that might be beyond him and that the Spirit of God never intended him to face. One plows and plants, another waters and weeds, and another garners and gleans. Let Mark recognize his limitations. It would be unkind to expose Mark to the kind of situation we faced at Lystra, for instance, where we were first worshiped and then stoned. I foresee rods and shipwreck. I foresee many journeys. I foresee perils of waters, perils of robbers, perils of our own countrymen, perils of heathen, perils in the city, perils in the wilderness, and perils among false brethren. I foresee weariness, pain, hunger, thirst, fastings, cold, and nakedness. I will not expose John Mark to these things—and that's that."

Who was right? Well, as in so many quarrels, both men were right and both were wrong. Barnabas parted company with Paul and the Holy Spirit left him to his choice and marched on with Paul.